MARRIAGE

Under Construction

for Women

ANGELA CASTILLO HERNANDEZ

LUIS HERNANDEZ

ISBN-13: 978-1539823094
ISBN-10: 1539823091

Edited by Jane Fisher
www.janefisheronline.com

Printed in the United States of America

Available for purchase at Amazon.com

DEDICATION

We dedicate this book to our parents, Miguel and Evelyn Castillo, and Irma Negron, for the years devoted to raising us with their best efforts and instilling values of love, family and relationship. We also dedicate this book to our other close family and friends who have shared life with us. But a special dedication goes to four wonderful men who are no longer with us, but were examples in our lives, in honor, respect, but above all, love. They are Hipolito Millet, Julio Castillo, Rogelio Nazario, and Pedro Feliciano.

CONTENTS

ACKNOWLEDGMENTS

First and foremost, we thank God for this amazing opportunity to touch marriages, and for the years of faithfulness in our lives. We thank Amy McClintock for her advice and insight as to how to even begin this project. She selflessly shared information just for the sake of helping. We also thank Jasmin Almodovar for her obedience in sharing with us the vision and word the Lord gave her, that we should begin the writing. We give a special thank you to our coach and editor of this project, Jane Fisher. She is truly an exceptional woman who is dedicated and cares about this work as though it was her own. Her insight and advice throughout this journey have been of great value. We could not have done this without her.

PREFACE

Thank you for choosing Marriage Under Construction! The book you have in your hands began as our notes for the marriage conference we present through Remodel Ministries. It has since grown to be both the conference guide for the attendees and a standalone book. We are amazed and humbled at how the Lord would use us in this fashion to touch the lives of so many people.

Although you will note that Angela speaks in the first person throughout the book, we wrote this book together as a couple, identifying the things the Lord has taught us through our 20 plus years of marriage. The book is written in the same casual tone used in the live conference, so that as far as possible, you have the feeling of being there with us.

There are two versions of the book, one for women and the other for men. Four of the chapters are the same in each book, which reflects the presentation of this material to the couples at the marriage conference. The purpose of the conference is to help couples grow closer together, and this is facilitated by receiving and discussing the information together.

In the third and fifth chapters, however, Luis speaks directly to men only, and Angela speaks directly to women only, again reflecting the marriage conference. The conference's split sessions allow husbands and wives an opportunity to speak candidly with only other men, or only other women, about the challenges and responsibilities of their different roles in the marriage.

This book is appropriate for individual or small group study, as well as a conference guide. Workbook pages are included, with both challenge questions based on the content written, and with many of the specific Bible verses that support the material. We encourage you to study the passages, and space is provided for notations.

We hope you will grow spiritually through these books, and pray for God's special blessings in your marriage.

Luis & Angela

Chapter One

BLUEPRINT

...whose architect and builder is God.
Hebrews 11:10, NIV

I was nineteen years old when Luis and I were married. I really had no idea what I was in store for. I saw what my parents' marriage looked like. I saw what the marriages of my relatives, family friends and couples from the church looked like. However, I really had no idea what marriage was. I was like every other young woman who dreamed of getting married to "The One." I only imagined being loved and taken care of.

My husband and I met and married in five months. We eloped, and we were so in love that we wanted nothing more than to spend our lives together. I thought we knew everything, and knew all we needed to know at that time. I wasn't prepared for what was coming next.

The Dream Becomes Reality

Shortly after marrying my husband, I realized that there was a lot more to marriage than I understood. I knew there would be disputes and difficulties. Nevertheless, I always assumed that it would be easy to navigate through, as long as there was enough love. I was wrong.

It wasn't easy, even with all the love I felt. There was difficulty in adjusting to my new life. I now had new responsibilities to take care of him. In addition to working and attending school, I had to cook, clean, do the laundry, take care of our children, and make sure that he had what he needed on a daily basis. I had to think about what he liked, and what he wanted. It was no longer just about me. I had to consider his thoughts and his preferences.

In the beginning, this wasn't a problem. In fact, I was so in love that I looked forward to doing things for him. I looked forward to pleasing him and doing my best to make him happy. But as time passed and disagreements set in, it wasn't so easy to do at times. It was difficult because after an argument or a dispute, I honestly didn't want to do anything for him. I really lacked motivation, especially in times when I felt disappointed that he wasn't doing things for me.

As a husband, Luis had similar feelings. He was responsible for more than just himself now and had to take care of me, as well.

List the things that you did to demonstrate your love for your spouse when you first got together. Do you still do any of these things today?

_____

_____

_____

_____

_____

_____

_____

_____

_____

_____

_____

_____

_____

_____

_____

_____

_____

_____

_____

_____

When we first started dating, he made every effort to impress me. He took pride in showing me how great of a man he was, and how much he could do for me. When disagreements began, he was less than motivated, just as I had been. I had disappointed him, too.

We quickly learned to be careful with what we said. Things that were never an issue before would stir up an argument. We were arguing about everything. It was frustrating because it didn't matter how small and ridiculous the issue was. We sought advice from my aunt or from our Pastor, and one of the things that we were advised, and knew the Bible said, was not to go to bed angry.

Let me just tell you that when we are angry or upset about something that one of us has done, we are not in the mood to fix anything, let alone sleep so nestled and cuddly with each other. We both had difficulty giving in and we both thought we were right. We each thought it was up to the other to apologize.

I felt that he was not meeting my expectations of what our marriage should be like. I thought, *How could he hurt me if he said he loves me? Doesn't he understand me? Doesn't he know what I expected of him? I haven't changed; I'm still the same person he dated. Is he oblivious? Why can't I do anything right?*

His thoughts were similar. *How could she say she loves me and not respect me? Doesn't she see all the sacrifices I am making? Doesn't she see how hard I am working for our family? I am a good, providing, and hard-working man. Doesn't she see that? What changed? She wasn't like this before.*

How have some of your expectations hurt your spouse?

...Do not let the sun go down while you are still angry, and do not give the devil a foothold.

Ephesians 4:26--27, NIV

We had issues with our families as well. I not only had to deal with all of his issues, but now I had to deal with his family, and he had to deal with mine. I loved his family, and he loved mine, but sometimes it seemed as though we both had too many things to prove to them. *Wasn't it enough that we chose to leave our families to start our own family? Didn't his family see my sacrifice; didn't my family see his?* All we both could think of was, *How could everything be so difficult after it was so great? Did we make a mistake?*

I felt trapped because I knew how the Lord felt about divorce. I did not want to have a failed marriage. What would that say to my family who believed in marriage? What would I tell our children?

I didn't have a dream of a failed marriage. I dreamed of happily ever after. I dreamed of celebrating 25 years, then 50 years of wedded bliss. Although I didn't want to have a failed marriage, I had conflicting information. The information I thought I knew through my religious beliefs, and views of marriage through examples, was different from information I knew the world was providing.

Luis did not have many examples of what marriage should be. In fact, in the beginning he thought that it was a valid option to just walk away from me. However, after Luis accepted Jesus Christ as his Lord and Savior, he also now knew what the Bible had to say and struggled with the same conflict.

The Miracle

Luis accepted the Lord after we faced one of the toughest moments in our life. Our first-born suffered an accident to his head and almost died at 5 months, due to internal bleeding. He survived, thankfully, but later that year he began to have seizures, and it was seriously out of control.

One day at home, after only arriving less than 20 minutes from being discharged from the hospital for his seizures, my son suffered another bad seizure. All we could do was hold him, watch him and wait for the seizure to pass, with prayers that this seizure would not be the one that would cause physical and permanent damage to his brain.

My husband, with tears in his eyes, looked at me and said, "What can we do so that this doesn't continue to happen to him?" In an instant, without even thinking about it, and with true conviction in my heart, I said, "You must accept the Lord Jesus Christ as your Savior, and I must ask for forgiveness and reconcile my life back to Him!"

That night, God gave a miracle in the life of my son. When I returned to the hospital, I prayed by his bedside. That night I gave my heart to the Lord. I pleaded with God to heal my son. I told God that I would serve Him no matter what, if He healed my son, or even if He didn't. I said I was sorry for turning my back on Him for so many years. I gave my heart to the Lord and was determined to serve Him no matter what happened.

The next day, all sorts of tests were performed in order to find an imbalance in his head. The doctors had diagnosed him with epilepsy. They had to run multiple tests to find out what specifically was happening to him. The test results came back, and what happened next was astonishing.

I was taken to a conference room filled with about eight doctors. They were all discussing my son's case. They were baffled because they couldn't understand why all the test results came back negative, with no signs of epilepsy. In my heart, I immediately knew what God had done.

The Problem

The next available Sunday we both gave our hearts to the Lord. We were both so grateful and had so much faith in who God is, because of what He did in our son's life. Now we wanted to make sure we obeyed Him in every aspect of our lives, including our marriage. However, it doesn't mean that it was any easier to deal with, or to do. So now, Luis faced my same dilemma.

Luis didn't grow up with his dad and did not want that for his children. He didn't want his children to feel the void he felt as a child. His father's example was always present in his mind, as well as what he learned in the Word of God. So we both struggled with the contrasting information between what the world said, and what the Bible taught about marriage.

You may be asking yourself, *What does she mean by "the world's view?" Who is "the world?"* When I talk about the world, I mean general society. A general society that doesn't follow what the Bible has to say, but follows the opinions and beliefs that are formed by a matter of opinion of the general population. In other words, in today's society, what is popular in the public eye or mainstream. Opinions about marriage that are contrary to God's Word have become popular view. You must make sure not to fall into those thoughts so that you're not led down the wrong path.

Something very popular to say is, "You only live once." Some other common clichés and well-known quotes are:

> *All life is an experiment. The more experiments you make the better.*
> —Ralph Waldo Emerson

> *If you obey all the rules, you'll miss all the fun.*
> —Katherine Hepburn

> *There is only one success, to be able to spend your life in your own way.*
> —Christopher Morley

> *Life has no limitations, except the ones you make.*
> —Les Brown

Most people believe these sayings, and see no harm in them.

However, if you look closer you can see from these common clichés, the view of the world is *self-gratification*. In this technologically enhanced era people want things bigger, bolder, better and faster. If it's not fast enough, self-indulgent enough, the best, or the biggest, then it's no good. Therefore, when I say "the world" you can now understand that I mean what is popular with the general population. These thoughts are contrary to what the Word of God says. The Word of God speaks about self-gratification in this way:

> *He died for everyone so that those who receive his new life will no longer live for themselves. Instead, they will live for Christ, who died and was raised for them.*
>
> **2 Corinthians 5:15, NLT**

What some may not understand is that we, as followers of Christ, believe that we should die to self and live for God. The world does not view this in the same way, but promotes the opposite, as you can tell from the common clichés mentioned. You can see it every day on television, in movies, in mainstream media and in other ways. However, the world doesn't come up with all these lies and thoughts on their own. Lies originate from Satan.

Describe what you've been taught about marriage and relationships from others and popular opinion.

_____

_____

_____

_____

_____

_____

_____

_____

_____

_____

_____

_____

Don't let anyone capture you with empty philosophies and high-sounding nonsense that come from human thinking and from the spiritual powers of this world, rather than from Christ.

Colossians 2:8, NLT

For the word of the Lord is right and true...

Psalms 33:4, NIV

...your word is truth.

John 17:17, NIV

Satan deceives the hearts and minds of people and infiltrates the world with these lies.

What do I mean by "lies" of Satan? The Word of God is the truth, therefore anything contrary to the Word of God is false or a lie. Satan formulates all lies, then he uses these lies to confuse our thoughts, and then it becomes part of the thoughts of society. You see an example of this in the Garden of Eden. When Satan approached Eve in the Garden, he lied to get her attention, and then continued to lie in order to confuse her and convince her.

> *Now the serpent was more crafty than any of the wild animals the Lord God had made. He said to the woman, "Did God really say, 'You must not eat from any tree in the garden'?"*
>
> **Genesis 3:1, NIV**

God didn't say that they must not eat from *any* tree. God specifically said from one very specific tree. So specific that He pointed the tree out by name.

> *And the Lord God commanded the man, "You are free to eat from any tree in the garden; but you must not eat from the tree of the knowledge of good and evil, for when you eat from it you will certainly die."*
>
> **Genesis 2:16—17, NIV**

What are some of the things you have learned from the Word of God concerning marriage.

_____

_____

_____

_____

_____

_____

_____

_____

_____

_____

_____

_____

_____

_____

_____

_____

...He [Satan] has always hated the truth, because there is no truth in him. When he lies, it is consistent with his character; for he is a liar and the father of lies.

John 8:44, NLT

Satan wanted to capture Eve's attention. He wanted to make the fruit of the tree appealing to her, in order to distract her from the truth, so that she and Adam would eventually sin and be separated from God.

Satan has been doing the same ever since. He lies to us in order to make things that are against God's Word seem appealing. He does this so that he can keep us separated from God's truth. His lies infiltrate into the thoughts of people who then feed the views of the world.

The World's View on Marriage

The world has much to say about knowing who your soulmate is, and what marriage should be. You're told that if your spouse doesn't live up to your expectations, then he or she must not be your real soulmate. The world tells you that you can abandon your spouse if you're not satisfied. The world's view of marriage is selfish, which makes the bond weak, powerless, and destructible.

When I speak with some people I know, who do not know the Lord, their mentality is that if your spouse is not fulfilling your desires, or your demands, or doing their part, then that person is a waste of your time. They'll tell you that he or she isn't the one for you because if they were, you wouldn't have so many struggles, they would understand who you are, and it would be much easier.

List any unrealistic expectations that you may have for your spouse.

In fact, they'll tell you, it is a waste of your time and you are too valuable to put up with anything less than what you deserve.

Watching old movies and television shows, if someone was about to get married, it would be for life. If they were in love with someone else, they would sort it out before they got married. Nowadays, there's no pressure to get it right ahead of time because divorce is acceptable now. Today's movies, television shows, and reality TV send the message that it is alright to get divorced.

The world feeds you this thought when entering marriage, "If it doesn't work out, you can just get a divorce." These types of thoughts contribute to many marriages that fail. From the beginning some may be entering the marriage with an escape plan. Even if someone enters marriage believing that the marriage will be for life, as I did, the moment things were not going your way, the thought of divorce enters your mind. These thoughts entered my mind, not because I wanted a divorce, but because I thought that things were so bad, that it was an option.

This thought process stems from selfishness. This isn't something that we can avoid completely. Unfortunately, we are imperfect humans and it's in our nature to be selfish. The main problem is *sin*. When Adam and Eve sinned, our communication with God and with each other was compromised. We'll discuss in further detail the ramifications of this in another session. However, the point here is that we are naturally selfish beings, and must try our best not to be that way.

The problem with fighting off selfishness is that it is contrary to the behaviors and thought processes that society promotes. Selfishness leads to disappointment, rejection, disapproval, anger, bitterness, isolation, and ultimately to marital destruction. This is mainly because there are two people in a marriage, which leaves no room for the selfish desires of one person. Not to ignore what your feelings and desires might be, but you must take into consideration another person, because now you share a life together.

This notion of finding the "one" or our "soulmate" is a myth. People selfishly searching for someone who is perfect for them, increases their expectations, which leads to many disappointments.

What to do Instead

Instead, you should seek the Lord's wisdom as to whom you should marry. Even then, it's impossible to completely avoid troubles with the person you marry. You can vet that person, spend time and properly plan, pray and seek wisdom before the wedding, and still have troubles, and at times feel as though you may have made a mistake. Expect that when you start to think that the person you married is not the right one, the enemy will use that to develop more thoughts of negativity toward your mate and your marriage. This is when it's essential that you understand that your troubles are not necessarily because you didn't find your perfect match.

Who's Your Soulmate?

Both partners in the marriage must work through the issues. You made a commitment to each other, before God, to give your entire self to the marriage. The woman becomes the one the husband must fight for; the man becomes the one the wife must fight for.

So don't think of marriage as finding someone who will be right for you. Approach marriage with the mindset that you'll do whatever you can to be right for your partner. And in the process, you will find that you don't marry the one. The person you marry *becomes* the one.

If you already read the Bible, you know that God tells His plan for how marriage should work. You do your best to work through any problems in your marriage, according to this plan.

There are those who accept the Lord after they marry, even though their spouse has not. The enemy tries to attack that marriage putting thoughts like these as well, using thoughts that he or she is not a believer and therefore now maybe there is an out. The Word tells us to honor these marriages if our spouse is willing.

Of course, there are some who try hard for their marriage, and it still doesn't work out. This could be for many reasons, and there is no condemnation to them. The reasons are between them and God. If they put their life in the Lord's hands and seek His will,

What are the ways you can show your spouse that you are fighting for your marriage?

_____

_____

_____

_____

_____

_____

_____

_____

_____

_____

_____

_____

_____

_____

For the unbelieving husband has been sanctified through his wife, and the unbelieving wife has been sanctified through her believing husband. Otherwise, your children would be unclean, but as it is, they are holy. But if the unbeliever leaves, let it be so. The brother or the sister is not bound in such circumstances; God has called us to live in peace.

1 Corinthians 7:14—15, NIV

God will bring fullness into their life in the manner that He knows is best and perfect for them. He loves them and desires nothing but the best for them.

My point here is to focus on those of you who want to work in your marriages today, and have a chance to strengthen or even save your marriage. About 33% of all marriages currently end in divorce[1] and that is only counting the people who actually got married legitimately. Imagine the number of couples that live together for years as a marriage (these were not counted as part of this study), and then split up. Although they weren't married legally, had they been, it would count as a divorce.

The world feeds you the idea that somehow if you didn't marry your soulmate, that it's alright to leave and continue searching. However, if you choose to believe with all your heart that the person you married *becomes* your soulmate - that they are the one person who is meant for you - you will work hard to save your marriage.

You'll work hard to ensure that you don't lose your spouse because you know that for you, there is no other one than he or she. The premise that if your partner doesn't meet your expectations, then it means that they aren't the right one after all, is

---

[1] Barna Group, Ventura, CA. (2008, March 31). *New Marriage and Divorce Statistics Released.* Retrieved August 03, 2016, from Barna: https://www.barna.org/barna-update/family-kids/42-new-marriage-and-divorce-statistics-released#.V6IQ8_krKCg

Describe ways that you can show your spouse that your marriage is important to you.

...A wife must not separate from her husband. But if she does, she must remain unmarried or else be reconciled to her husband. And a husband must not divorce his wife.

1 Corinthians 7:10-11, NIV

one of the many lies that Satan has filtered into the world, and it has ultimately influenced the church.

50/50

Another misconception is that marriage is a 50/50 proposition. I know this proposition all too well. When my husband and I were first married, we both did our best to please one another. In fact, part of the reason why we wanted to be together was because of how much we did for each other. To each of us, it showed how much we mattered to the other person. I remember thinking, "Wow! He is so sweet, so kind, and would do anything for me." He had me hooked! When we first dated, we were practically kids. I was only 19, and he was 22. We were both young and inexperienced, but thought we knew it all. We thought we had everything figured out.

Shortly after we were married, reality started to set in. We both had the desire to please one another, but it was impossible to do all the time. Then children and responsibilities of work and the house started to set in, and all of a sudden, we had less time with each other. We were tired from everyday life and responsibilities and had no desire to also, then do for one another. We started to argue about who did what, and who did not. Who did more, and who did less. We began to measure each other up. We began to try to keep track of how much we were giving to the relationship, and

Have you thought about the 50/50 concept in your marriage? What are things you have stopped doing that you used to do when you first got together?

_____

_____

_____

_____

_____

_____

_____

_____

_____

_____

_____

_____

_____

_____

_____

_____

_____

Serve wholeheartedly, as if you were servicing the Lord, not people,

Ephesians 6:7, NIV

how little we thought the other was contributing. We began to argue that the other partner wasn't giving their full 50%.

The problem with this notion is that it's not really possible to measure someone else's amount of effort. How do you know when the person has done their 50%? You shouldn't be measuring what the other person is giving, but instead focus on your own contribution to the marriage. In marriage, each person should give 100% without trying to measure what the other is giving. This is true even when one spouse is doing all the giving. How so?

You should be doing everything as though you are doing it for the Lord. You should be investing all your efforts into your marriage. I know it can be difficult sometimes, especially when you feel that your spouse is being particularly difficult. However, this is what the Lord commands us to do. The beautiful thing about this is that when you are obedient to God, even when it's hard, God will honor you for your actions.

Fix Yourself

One beautiful way the Lord may honor you in this, is that He will work in the heart of your spouse. If you look deeper into Colossians 3:23-24 (page 25), it states that you will get a reward from the Lord and He will give you what you should receive. If you combine this with the premise that you will reap what you sow

Do you find that you do things for your spouse out of obligation, or do you do them because you're pleased to do so?

Whatever work you do, do it with all your heart. Do it for the Lord and not for men. Remember that you will get your reward from the Lord. He will give you what you should receive. You are working for the Lord Christ.

Colossians 3:23—24, NLV

(Galatians 6:7), you can infer that as you honor the Lord with your obedience and invest all your efforts into the marriage, you will reap the reward of the Lord working in your spouse. Your focus should be on yourself and on doing your very best and the Lord will take care of all the rest.

It is not your job to change your spouse. Actually, didn't you marry your spouse for who they were, defects and all? Yes, you did. Are you perfect? No, you are not.

My assumption is that you thought your spouse was the greatest, and you wanted nothing more but to be with him or her. You dreamed of building a life together. But when things start getting difficult, you can forget. I forgot. I forgot why I wanted to be with my husband. All of a sudden, I started to see all of his faults. I questioned myself as to why I didn't notice before. Thankfully, God revealed to me that I was not all that perfect. I had many flaws of my own, as Luis was discovering. I was so wrapped up in what I thought I deserved from him—what I needed and what I wanted—that I forgot about *him*.

You can sometimes get so immersed in the world's view, believing that you somehow deserve to receive everything you want, that you give your spouse the job to fulfill your every wish. That type of thinking is grossly inappropriate. How could you expect a simple human to fulfill your every desire and your every need? That would unreasonable. Ask yourself, do you have the ability to do that for your spouse? I am sure that you will find that

List some reasons why you fell in love with your spouse.

you do not, and you shouldn't expect that from your spouse. The only one who can fill our every need is the Lord. Instead of doing for your spouse only if he or she is living up to their 50%, try always giving 100%. Anything else is selfish ambition.

What's Important

You are to value your spouse, and to serve your spouse not *selfishly*, but *selflessly*. Imagine the impact on your marriage if each of you had this type of attitude. If you would put the interests of your spouse above your own? You would see his or her dedication to the marriage, and it would inspire each of you to do more for each other. If only one of you starts at first, you can still motivate your spouse to give 100%, if you are leading by example.

Selfishness robs the marriage of communication, relationship, intimacy and romance, and leads to weakness. It wasn't easy for me to grasp this concept. Actually, it was quite difficult. I knew I had to serve my husband. Even though I didn't want to, or think he deserved it. I had to put my selfish desires aside and put him first. *Was this always easy to do?* No. It was not. In fact, I failed miserably many times, but had to stay strong and always try.

Luis also tried, but at first, I couldn't see what he was doing, because I was so focused on my own needs, and was looking for specific behavior changes.

What can you do for your spouse to make their day better?

Do nothing out of selfish ambition or vain conceit. Rather, in humility value others above yourselves, not looking to your own interests but each of you to the interests of the others.
Philippians 2:3—4, NIV

I remember praying and seeking the Lord's guidance. In that prayer, I did a lot of complaining. I complained about everything I was doing; I complained about all that Luis was not doing. I wondered when God was going to finally step in.

Then one morning, there was a prayer union in my church. I was on my way to work, but decided to go there instead to pray for my marriage. As I was arriving, I looked up and there were my husband and my best friend arriving at the church as well. He had asked her for advice on what he could do to better our marriage, and showed up to the church to pray for me and our marriage. I was so surprised and filled with so much joy, that I cried. Throughout the time I was selfishly complaining, my husband was actually trying in his own way.

I didn't notice it at first, but that day God confirmed to me that He was working in Luis, and I had to be patient. He confirmed that I was not perfect. He had to do changes in me, as well.

What I also learned was that the same way God loves me, God loves my husband, and that He will do what is best for both of us, if we both trust in Him. I was so focused on my own needs that I forgot that Luis had needs as well. Luis saw my dedication, but I failed to see his. Through prayer and seeking God's guidance, I was able to hear God's voice that morning so that He could confirm all that He was doing for me. It is very easy to feel depressed or get down if you're not careful. You must pray and ask for God's wisdom and strength, and that He will give you courage.

Focusing on our own needs could make us under-appreciate our spouse and cause sadness or make us feel weak. This is a time Satan could attack with various types of temptation. Write a prayer that can help you get through it.

Watch and pray so that you will not fall into temptation. The spirit is willing, but the flesh is weak.

Matthew 26:41, NIV

Thankfully, I knew the Lord, and through years of praying, years of devotion, years of studying His Word, years of drawing closer to the Lord, and years of working through mistakes and seeking wisdom concerning marriage, I was able to understand God's plan for marriage. His design. His purpose.

This took time to know, and it took devotion and willpower to fight for my marriage, and to fight to do what was right in God's eyes. In order to do that, I had to draw closer to Him. I had to first understand God's design for marriage. I had to put aside my dreams and societal beliefs of what marriage is and what it is not. I also had to put aside societal theories of why marriages fail or why some marriages were not meant to be. I had to look at what God said marriage is supposed to be. Then I had to accept that my marriage was not reflecting God's design, and decide that I needed to do everything in my power to change that.

God's Plan & Purpose

My marriage had to go *under construction*. I had to go back to the drawing board. What happens when you have a construction project? When you begin a project or "go back to the drawing board," you have to start out by drawing up the designs. You have to begin with blueprints.

When I decided to let my marriage go under construction, I had to allow God's blueprint and design to be reflected in my marriage. In order to do that, I had to allow God to enter into *all* areas of my life and my marriage. I had to allow Him to show me what *His* design was, and allow Him to be the Architect of my life, my marriage, and my family.

So what exactly does it mean when I say God's blueprint and design? God's blueprint and design are His purpose and plan for marriage. The Bible illustrates God's purpose and plan for marriage this way:

> *As the Scriptures say, " A man leaves his father and mother and is joined to his wife, and the two are united into one." This is a great mystery, but it is an illustration of the way Christ and the church are one.*
>
> **Ephesians 5:31—32, NLT**

God planned for man and woman to be united into one flesh. They are to leave their parents to build a life together. If you think about how deep this is, you will understand how great this is. Your parents gave you life. They nurtured and cared for you. They taught you and prepared you. In other words, they provided such a big service to you so that you could become the adults you need to be. Even after all of this, God says to leave them. God says to leave them in order to be married, in order to form a new family.

The parents He said to honor are the ones you must leave, and now your focus should be your spouse. Not that you should ever stop honoring your parents. But now you have a covenant with your spouse. The Word of God states that this is a great mystery and compares it to the way Christ and the church are one. Christ has a covenant with you, and you have a covenant with your spouse. A covenant is an agreement, a contract, and a bond. This is a great testimony to what a true marriage should encompass. Marriage is designed to be a reflection of your relationship with Christ.

Your marriage should testify to the world the love that Christ has for the church. Christ and the church are one, and so are you in your marriages. When you love God, and truly want to do His will, you then realize that your marriage should testify to the way your relationship should be with the Lord. You also realize the importance of working through your marriage and making it be the reflection that God wants it to be. This is true even as individuals. You need to understand that God made you in His image.

Marriage was not intended to satisfy your own needs and desires. Marriage is much bigger than that. This is the reason that Satan attacks marriages. God intended for marriage partners to operate as one unit in order to bring forth spiritually, mentally and emotionally sound individuals. When Satan attacks marriages, he is trying to bring down the human race and separate them from God's plan. A marriage operating as designed testifies to God's

Do you believe that you have shown your spouse your true commitment? What are some things that you can do to demonstrate your commitment?

_____

_____

_____

_____

_____

_____

_____

_____

_____

_____

_____

_____

_____

_____

_____

So God created mankind in his own image, in the image of God he created them; male and female he created them. God blessed them and said to them, "Be fruitful and increase in number; fill the earth and subdue it..."

Genesis 1:27—28, NIV

glory, and promotes God's plan for healthy families, who then also breed healthy future marriages.

Marriage should be operating as one flesh in order to succeed. Becoming "one flesh" is not just through getting married or having sex. This is a process. It doesn't happen overnight. It takes devotion, dedication, and prayer to achieve unity. Then it takes devotion, dedication, and prayer for each spouse to empower the other to live in this unity. It is important that we understand that we were not meant to be alone.

Adam saw that there was none suitable for him. The Hebrew word for suitable is "kenegdo," meaning "equal." God Himself saw that it was not good for man to be alone, and therefore made the woman as his equal. God did not intend for a woman to be seen as less than a man.

Together "ezer kenegdo," translated into "suitable helper," really translates into an equal rescuer, an equal strength, and equal help. The woman was not made inferior. Of course, God gave each of us a role. Yes, you are to respect your husband as the head of the household. However, this is not because you are inferior. On the contrary, every leader needs a strong helper, and every leader is unable to do all things on their own.

I believe that God's making Eve from Adam's rib is an example of how man and woman belong together as one. It was not good for man to be alone, there was no one suitable for him, and he was in need of a helper. However, woman was made from

The Lord God said, "It is not good for the man to be alone. I will make a helper suitable for him."

Now the Lord God had formed out of the ground all the wild animals and all the birds in the sky. He brought them to the man to see what he would name them; and whatever the man called each living creature, that was its name. So the man gave names to all the livestock, the birds in the sky and all the wild animals.

But for Adam no suitable helper was found. So the Lord God caused the man to fall into a deep sleep; and while he was sleeping, he took one of the man's ribs and then closed up the place with flesh.

Then the Lord God made a woman from the rib he had taken out of the man, and he brought her to the man.

The man said,

"This is now bone of my bones
and flesh of my flesh;
she shall be called 'woman,'
for she was taken out of man."

That is why a man leaves his father and mother and is united to his wife, and they become one flesh."

Genesis 2:18—23, NIV

the man, to show her need for him as well. The fact that God chose to make the woman from a man, instead of forming the woman from dust alone, shows His idea of what our relationship with one another should be. It demonstrates our need for one another in our marriages.

He made woman from the rib, which is a part of the body that is on the side, to show how comparable they should be. The rib is under Adam's arm to show the protection and love women are to receive from their husbands. Also, the rib is a bone that protects the most vital and important organs, demonstrating the important role wives have in protecting (ezer) their husbands as well.

Adam was enthusiastic when he saw Eve. Adam understood that Eve was a gift. He stated that she is "bone of his bone and flesh of his flesh," so he understood the significance, and how precious she was. He understood that because she came out of him, he was to receive her as his own flesh and join to her as one.

When a man and woman join their lives together, they both should acknowledge their need for one another. Both should acknowledge their spouse as a gift. The marriage will only be successful if *both* acknowledge this and give to each other the love, respect, and honor they each require. When one spouse fails to do this, it can be detrimental to the relationship.

Husbands—understand that your wife is good. Notice that Proverbs 18:22 (page 39) does not say, "He who finds a *good* wife;

What are some ways that you can show your spouse that you value them in your life?

_____

_____

_____

_____

_____

_____

_____

_____

_____

_____

_____

_____

_____

_____

_____

_____

He who finds a wife finds what is good and receives favor from the Lord.

Proverbs 18:22, NIV

it simply says "a wife." The wife that God has given you as a gift is good, and she is a gift from the Lord.

Wives—your husband is a gift to you as well. You were designed to be his helper, his companion, because it wasn't good for him to be alone. Remember that you were specially made. Therefore, a wife must honor God and His love for her husband and man must love and honor his wife.

In Summary

This plan, this blueprint, this design that God intended is not always easy to grasp. However, if you choose to follow God's plan instead of the world's pattern, you will find that it can be a great blessing for your marriage.

If you now know what God's blueprint and design are for your marriage, it is up to you individually to do all you can to allow His design and plan to be the ruler of your actions. You must follow all that He has in store for you. Not only will it be a blessing for you, but it will be a blessing for your spouse and your children. God is the Architect, has designed and made a blueprint, and you must choose to accept that blueprint and build your lives according to His design. There is much more to His plan and design.

We will discover together in the following chapters how everything fits into His design. All the steps and pieces, just as you would find in a construction project. The design alone is simply

Describe how you can change to reflect God's plan for marriage in your life.

_____

_____

_____

_____

_____

_____

_____

_____

_____

_____

_____

_____

_____

_____

_____

_____

_____

_____

not enough to make something beautiful, there are steps and other workings that follow in order to make a design come to life. God supplies us with the design and all the tools we need in order to make our marriages become what He has planned for us.

It can be difficult, but it is possible. Not in our own strength, but with His strength. God loves His children and wants nothing but beauty in their lives. My marriage is far from perfect, but it is better today than it was yesterday, and will be better tomorrow than today. I may not know all the secrets and I am growing daily. But one thing that I know with all my heart is that if I trust God, and obey His commands, that He will put everything in its place, and this includes my marriage, my children, my family, and my friends. His design, His blueprint is better than anything that I can design or plan for. Let's work on this project together, discovering all of the wonderful joys that the Lord has for us.

Chapter One - Discussion Questions

Prior to reading this chapter, what did you believe was the purpose of your marriage? If your belief changed, in what ways did it change?

Chapter One – Take Action!

Compare your answer to the question on page 43, with that of your husband's answer on men's page 43. Plan the ways that you both will contribute to your marriage, so that you will live according to God's blueprint.

_____

_____

_____

_____

_____

_____

_____

_____

_____

_____

_____

_____

_____

Chapter Two

FOUNDATION

Look! I am placing a foundation stone...
a precious cornerstone that is safe to build on...
Isaiah 28:16, NLT

O nce you receive the blueprints that were drawn and designed by the Architect for your marriage, then the actual work begins. This is a construction project and each step is important in the process. Each task should be completed without taking any shortcuts. Once Luis and I knew what God's design was, we each had to work hard to follow it.

With any project, after the plans are drawn, the first crucial step is the laying down of the foundation. If the foundation is not done correctly, everything in the rest of the project is compromised. A building project is built and sits on its foundation, just as your entire relationship will sit on the foundation you set for your marriage.

I found out very quickly that the most important part of my life and my marriage was my communication, relationship, and connection with God. Christ should be at the center of our lives and our marriages. All the truths that we have learned, and all that He has shown us through His grace and mercy, was only possible to recognize through communication with Him.

For Luis it is the same. That day when we both found ourselves at the church prayer meeting, ready to talk to God and pray for each other, was a breakthrough for us. Not only did it show me that my husband cared enough for our marriage, and for me, to go to God about it, it also showed me that it was the only way I was going to be the best that I can be. It showed me that it was the only way we were going to have success in our marriage.

I am such a perfectionist. I am always trying to plan properly. I am always trying to make sure that everything comes out right. I am very detail-oriented and look to make the best plans possible. It was difficult for me to relinquish my control because I liked being in control. I always thought I was right; this is a trait that we women may often struggle with.

I had to learn to give it all to God to control. In order for me to do that, I had to start by acknowledging my need for God in my life, and then try to follow Him the best way I could. I had to build a relationship with the Lord by continuously communicating with Him. Luis had to do the same. However, as much as it is difficult

What are some things that you have to surrender to the Lord?

for me to admit, Luis had a better time in this area because he was more willing to give control to God.

We both had to build communication with the Lord. It is only through communication with Him, that we can hear from Him. *How can we obey someone we cannot hear? How can we know what to do if we cannot receive the instructions?* Our primary foundation is communication. First build communication with God, and then build communication with each other.

Communication With God

If you want to have a healthy, successful marriage, you first need to start with yourself. You cannot possibly be your best self without allowing God into your life to help you. In order to do this, you need to build a personal relationship with Him.

It's important to understand that God loves you. His love is the rebar in the concrete of your marriage's foundation; the structure that strengthens our relationship with God. The enemy tries to weaken your relationship with God by putting doubt in your mind concerning God's love for you.

God loves you. Christ came and died on the cross to redeem us all. He loved you first, and His love doesn't change, no matter what condition you are in. The enemy tells you the lie that you are no good, or not good enough for God's love. Many people hold themselves back from even trying to have a relationship with God

List several things you can do to build your communication with God.

_____

_____

_____

_____

_____

_____

_____

_____

_____

_____

_____

_____

_____

_____

_____

For this is how God loved the world: He gave his one and only Son, so that everyone who believes in him will not perish but have eternal life

John 3:16, NLT

We love because he first loved us.

1 John 4:19, ESV

because they feel that they would never be good enough. One of the many sayings that I have heard is, "If I were to go to church, the church would collapse". Some are so hard on themselves that they deny themselves a new start, and deny themselves a wonderful life in the Lord. If that is you, do not let the enemy continue to lie to you in this way.

> *but God shows his love for us in that while we were still sinners, Christ died for us.*
>
> **Romans 5:8, ESV**

Christ chose to give His life for you even though you are a sinner. He loves you regardless of who you are and what you've done. Satan will try to convince you that you are beyond loving, and will try to make you feel guilty about your past. Satan will try to bring constant condemnation to your life. We have all messed up. We have all committed sin, and we all have failed the Lord.

But, God loves you so much that He sent His son to die for you, so that you might have new life in Him. He offers forgiveness through Christ and His sacrifice. You only have to accept His sacrifice and accept Christ into your heart.

God gives you the right to become His child when you accept the sacrifice that Christ made. When you believe and ask for forgiveness, He gives righteousness in exchange for your sins. When you accept Christ in your life as your Savior, you are made

Compose an affirmation that describes how God loves you.

_____

_____

_____

_____

_____

_____

_____

_____

_____

_____

_____

_____

_____

For everyone has sinned: we all fall short of God's glorious standard.

Romans 3:23, NLT

But to all who believed him and accepted him, he gave the right to become children of God.

John 1:12, NLT

Therefore, if anyone is in Christ, he is a new creation; old things have passed away; behold, all things have become new.2
Corinthians 5:17, NKJV

brand new; you are a new creation. God offers you a new life. Be confident knowing that God will not only make you brand new, but He will forgive and forget all of your sins. His saving grace is a wonderful right that is a gift to you; you can't take credit for it. You just have to be willing to accept the gift, willing to turn off the lies that you hear about God's love and forgiveness.

If you have not accepted Christ as your Savior, or have not been living in relationship with Him, you can freely ask Christ into your heart, tell Him that you accept His sacrifice on the cross, and now want to have a life with Him in it. It is that simple to begin. You are invited to create a relationship with Him by intentionally getting to know God through prayer, worship and His Word.

Another reason Christ gave His life on the cross was so that your communication with Him would no longer be limited. In the Old Testament, only the High Priest was allowed to approach the dwelling place of God in the temple. The design of the temple included a large curtain to create a separation from the people, and even the High Priest was only allowed in this area once a year.

When Christ gave His life on the cross, this curtain in the temple was torn.

"At that moment the curtain of the temple was torn in two from top to bottom..."
Matthew 27:51, NIV

Think about what your prayer life looks like. Write down some things that may need changing.

_____

_____

_____

_____

_____

_____

_____

_____

_____

_____

_____

_____

_____

_____

_____

For I will forgive their wickedness and will remember their sins no more.

Hebrews 8:12, NIV

God saved you by his grace when you believed. And you can't take credit for this; it is a gift from God

Ephesians 2:8, NLT

The significance of the torn curtain was that there was no longer a barrier between God and you. You can now go to our Lord freely in prayer and speak to Him. There is no need for someone to do this on your behalf. You have a direct line of communication to your Father in Heaven.

How wonderful that one of the first things that happened after Christ gave His life on the cross was that direct communication with God was encouraged. In my opinion, this shows how much God wanted a relationship with you, that the curtain was one of the first physical things that were discarded when Christ gave His life.

Once you've established communication with God, you're able to hear from Him, and learn to recognize His voice. It's important to obey what He says. Your life depends on this truth.

Everyone then who hears these words of mine and does them will be like a wise man who built his house on the rock. And the rain fell, and the floods came, and the winds blew and beat on that house, but it did not fall, because it had been founded on the rock. And everyone who hears these words of mine and does not do them will be like a foolish man who built his house on the sand. And the rain fell, and the floods came, and the winds blew and beat against that house, and it fell, and great was the fall of it.

Matthew 7:24-27, ESV

List some of the things that you know God is telling you to do in your relationship with Him.

_____

_____

_____

_____

_____

_____

_____

_____

_____

_____

_____

_____

_____

_____

_____

_____

My sheep listen to my voice; I know them, and they follow me.
John 10:27, NLT

These verses express the importance of building your life foundation on Christ. If you build your life on Christ, nothing can shake you in any area of your life, including your marriage.

However, if you don't, your personal life, and everything else, will be demolished because the foundation was not built correctly. Your foundation in the Lord should be built through prayer and His Word. It is important that you do this to become the men and women God intended you to be. If you build your marriage on Christ, you are sure that nothing can break it.

It is important that both spouses take part in this foundation. A marriage has two people, and both need to do their best for the other. It is foolish to build your house on the sand, and not the rock. It is foolish to build your marriage on anything else that is not Christ, who is the Rock! It is foolish to hear from God, know His Word and not follow His instruction.

One of the important ways you communicate with God is through prayer. "Prayer," as defined in the dictionary[2], is "an address (as a petition) to God or a god in word or thought, or an earnest request or wish." It is so great that you have someone to present your requests to.

---

[2]*Merriam-Webster.com.* (2015). Retrieved September 7, 2016, from Merriam-Webster: http://www.merriam-webster.com/dictionary/prayer

Write a prayer for your marriage.

"do not be anxious about anything, but in everything by prayer and supplication with thanksgiving let your requests be made known to God."

Philippians 4:6, ESV

Prayer is simply speaking to God, and God allows you to bring your petitions to Him. He cares about what your needs and desires are because He loves you. You just have to be willing to talk to Him. Talk to Him at all times, and about everything.

God wants constant communication with you. The best thing about this is that you do not have to pretend to be anybody else; you can be yourself because God already knows you. Something awesome is that you don't need eloquent words. All you need to do is open up your mind, your heart, and speak to God. He is ready, willing and able to listen to you. You will never bother Him.

God knew you before you were even formed in the womb. You can express yourself freely without any fear, transparently, at any time and from any place. Be open and honest. This is the best way to have communication with God.

Communication does not only involve talking, it also involves listening. Just as you need to talk to God, you need to listen to Him. God will speak to you in different ways. However, the best way He'll speak to you is through His Word.

Write a personal petition to the Lord.

_____
_____
_____
_____
_____
_____
_____
_____
_____
_____
_____
_____
_____
_____

pray without ceasing; give thanks in all circumstances; for this is the will of God in Christ Jesus for you.

1 Thessalonians 5:17-18, ESV

Before I formed you in the womb I knew you.

Jeremiah 1:5, ESV

All Scripture is inspired by God and is useful to teach us what is true and to make us realize what is wrong in our lives. It corrects us when we are wrong and teaches us to do what is right.

2 Timothy 3:16, NLT

God gives you His Word to teach you, to help you, and to speak to you. Through the help of the Holy Spirit, you are able to understand what God has to say to you in His Word. When you pray and meditate on His Word, God reveals to you what He wants you to know. Your communication with Him is not one-sided; you speak to Him, and He speaks back. He listens to us, and you should listen back. Communication takes both individuals to work.

In order to make communication work, there has to be trust. You can absolutely trust God. He knows you better than you know yourself. He knows what is best for you. He loves you. He sacrificed Himself for you. The trust you should have in the Lord is greater than any other trust you can have. Trust, transparency, and devotion are very important to developing your relationship.

You will find that after you've started to build communication with the Lord, the communication you build with your spouse is a bit easier, too. This is mainly because both of you are trying to be better versions of yourselves out of obedience to God. By being better versions of yourselves, you are able to be better to each other. This does not mean that you'll be perfect, or won't make any

What are some things that you can honestly say that you have not entrusted God fully with? You have tried giving, but still hold on to?

_____
_____
_____
_____
_____
_____
_____
_____
_____
_____
_____
_____
_____
_____

Trust in the Lord with all your heart...

Proverbs 3:5, NKJV

Blessed is the man who trusts in the Lord, And whose hope is the Lord.

Jeremiah 17:7, NKJV

mistakes. All are imperfect; however, you are instructed by the Word to continue forward and to imitate Christ. Therefore, you are striving to be better versions of yourself by obeying the Lord.

Obeying the Lord helps you to treat one another with love. This was one of His greatest commandments. Jesus Himself declared which were the two most important commandments.

Teacher, which is the great commandment in the Law?" And he said to him, "You shall love the Lord your God with all your heart and with all your soul and with all your mind. This is the great and first commandment. And a second is like it: You shall love your neighbor as yourself. On these two commandments depend all the Law and the Prophets.
Matthew 22:36-40, ESV

When you begin to follow these two commands, you not only build communication with the Lord, but then you begin to build communication with each other. You should love each other as you love yourselves. In order to love each other as you love yourselves, you must know each other through communication.

Communication with Each Other

While the first part of the foundation is communication with God, communication with each other comes next. Better communication with each other will support and strengthen other areas of your marriage. These include better relationship, resolving conflict, sexual intimacy, decision-making and others. Sharing with each other is the first step to communication.

Just like when communicating with God, you must be transparent with each other. After the Lord, your spouse should be the person you are most transparent with. You both should feel free to share your feelings, concerns, joys, etc., with each other.

> *Now the man and his wife were both naked, but they felt no shame.*
>
> **Genesis 2:25, NLT**

There should be no shame, even in your most vulnerable moments. Both spouses should absolutely share with each other, but sharing requires trust. Married individuals, have such a special relationship with each other. Your spouse sees and knows you in an intimate way that others do not. To develop this vital trust, both partners must prove themselves worthy of trust by not being judgmental with each other, and by keeping private matters private.

With love, there is no fear; no fear means there is trust. You have to vigilantly protect your spouse's trust, in order to keep an open channel to freely communicate with each other. Free communication can be life changing, and marriage saving.

Because of the communication I share with my husband, I am able to understand him better. Through many years of marriage, I had to learn more about my husband, how he grew up, and the experiences he went through. Learning of how he grew up and his earlier experiences, helped me to be more understanding in times that I necessarily didn't agree with how he was acting, or handling things. Luis learning of mine did the same for him.

I previously stated that God knows you and understands you better than you know yourself, but it is not the same for your spouse. Your spouse needs to learn about you in order to understand you. This only comes through communication, through trust, and sharing freely. Your spouse cannot read your mind, or even pretend to know how you feel about something unless you share this with them first.

However, when you are sharing and expressing yourself, you should make sure that you don't offend your spouse. Take your partner's feelings into consideration. Make sure you think about what you are sharing or saying. Make sure the timing is right.

> *Everyone enjoys a fitting reply; it is wonderful to say the right thing at the right time!*
> **Proverbs 15:23, NLT**

Another important thing to keep in mind is that sometimes there are feelings that do not need to be expressed. Don't misunderstand what I'm saying. You should be open and free with

Have you shown your spouse that you can be trusted? What are some ways you can show your spouse that you are there for them, and that they can trust you?

_____

_____

_____

_____

_____

_____

_____

_____

_____

_____

_____

_____

_____

_____

There is no fear in love. But perfect love drives out fear, because fear has to do with punishment. The one who fears is not made perfect in love."

1 John 4:18, NIV

one another. Sometimes your spouse may not be ready to receive something you want to share. Sometimes it may do more harm than good. You need to use prudence with what you are sharing.

When words are many, transgression is not lacking, but whoever restrains his lips is prudent.
Proverbs 10:19, ESV

The one you need to be the freest with is the Lord. The Lord is always willing to listen; some things just need to be taken to Him. Timing in what to say, and when to say it, can mean a difference between understanding and misunderstanding.

The art of expression and exchanging of information, ideas, thoughts and feelings are key concepts when it comes to communication. However, in order for the expression and exchanging of information to be effective, the other party has to be listening.

You have to listen to each other. It is good to share, but one person doing all the sharing is not good enough, and one person doing all the listening is not good enough either.

Sometimes one person in the marriage can be the one who always likes to talk. While it is good to be a person who likes to share all the time, the person always talking can sometimes overpower the other person's ability to also share. This can even cause poor communication lines to shut down completely.

Are you sharing with your spouse? Have you been mindful of their feelings? Self-evaluate how you share with your spouse.

_____

_____

_____

_____

_____

_____

_____

_____

_____

_____

_____

_____

_____

_____

_____

For everything there is a season, and a time for every matter under heaven:

Ecclesiastes 3:1, ESV

...A time to keep silence, and a time to speak;

Ecclesiastes 3:7, ESV

The ability to listen can help to strengthen communication in marriage. The Word of God tells you that you should be quick to hear and slow to speak. You need to make sure that one person is not doing all the talking. Both have to listen to each other speak, meaning the person who is not the talkative one will have to give the other person the opportunity to listen to you speak.

Listening involves more than just being quiet. Listening involves being engaged with what the other is saying.

...listen to me, and be attentive to the words of my mouth.

Proverbs 7:24, ESV

There has to be a genuine interest in what the other person is saying. You must listen to all that person has to say and not only focus on what may interest you, or what offends or upsets you. That is called selective listening. Selective listening can damage the communication lines.

A good listener will make the other person feel that his or her voice or concerns are important. There also has to be respect for their point of view or interest. You may not agree, but you can still learn to respect their view.

Active listening increases your understanding of each other, which helps to build stronger communication. The adjective definition of the word "understanding," is to be sympathetically

Are you listening to your spouse? Have you been mindful of what they may want to share? Self-evaluate how you listen to your spouse.

You must be quick to listen, slow to speak...

James 1:19, NLT

aware of other people's feelings; tolerant and forgiving. Understanding involves compassion. Sometimes it may be difficult for you to understand your spouse. Especially when you might not agree with something that he or she is expressing.

Although this can be difficult, it is possible to overcome. You have to be intentional about listening with understanding. If you do not understand something, ask questions. The best sign of listening is asking specific questions about what that person is sharing. Ask questions that clarify what your spouse is saying. For example, if your spouse said, "I saw the car", and you want more information, you can ask, "What color was the car you saw?" I know this is a simple example, but if you notice, the question was specific about the car that was mentioned. This can help you to understand more completely what your spouse is sharing. It can help your spouse feel as though you are engaged and care about what they are sharing. This can be beneficial for both spouses.

However, some questions can cause contention. It is beneficial to listen with a positive attitude. If the speaker doesn't carefully choose their words, they could offend unintentionally. If this happens, first assume that they have good intentions, and ask for clarification before jumping to any wrong conclusions.

Luis and I have completely different styles of communicating. I naturally like to talk and like to teach. Since I was a child, I've felt compelled to help those in class struggling with schoolwork. I was a good student, but every year the teachers would write in the comment section of my report card, "Angela is a great student, but she talks too much, she must remember that she is not the teacher." Talking and trying to teach others is part of my personality. As a child, a teenager, and a mother it was fine. However, as a wife, this can be damaging.

There were times that Luis and I were discussing certain issues or topics, and if I thought Luis didn't understand my view, I would ask, "Do you know what the word so and so means". This would stir up an argument. Where I was trying to help him to understand what I was saying, he took my question as though I was actually talking down to him, as though he could not understand the words I was using.

Several things were wrong here. First, I did this sort of thing many times, and many times, I got the same type of response. The number one thing I had to learn was that although I did not mean harm in what I was saying, I was offending him. After the first argument that we had when I used this type of method, I should have tried another approach.

Luis also needed to learn to listen positively. Instead of receiving my question negatively and assuming that I was talking down to him, if he had a positive attitude and chose to believe that I would not intentionally offend him, he would have realized that I was just trying to explain what I meant.

Because he was taking his time to answer, and because he was asking certain questions, I would assume he did not understand. If

I expected a certain reaction or response, I would get frustrated that he did not understand me, and then proceed into teaching mode. I needed to be positive as well, and have patience. I had to wait and receive his full response before I decided that he did not understand me.

The most important lesson in this example is that Luis and I have two different styles of expression. We express ourselves differently and both of us needed to learn one another's style of expression. Just to summarize some of our styles of expression, I am open, talkative and like to be helpful and to respond quickly. Luis is more to himself, a man with not so many words; he only likes to respond if needed, and only when he has full information about the entire situation.

Learning each other's style was not an overnight process. This takes years and dedication to one another. It also takes desire. You will not learn about your spouse unless you desire to do so. Desire leads to effort, effort leads to understanding.

By wisdom a house is built,
and by understanding it is established.

Proverbs 24:3, ESV

We both had to learn not to think or act with our emotions. You cannot go based on your feelings all the time. Your feelings can get you into trouble. Depending on your emotional state for

What are some of the things you can work on when you communicate with your spouse?

_____

_____

_____

_____

_____

_____

_____

_____

_____

_____

_____

_____

_____

_____

_____

_____

_____

the day, you can perceive things that may not necessarily be correct. Our emotions can be deceptive. Try to focus on what your spouse is trying to communicate, and not necessarily how it may be said or how you believe it came across.

If you are the communicator, try to break bad communication habits. Communicate clearly, do not leave things open to interpretation. Watch your tone of voice, your facial expressions, body language, or hand movements. Sometimes the listener is doing everything possible to be engaging and non-judgmental but your communication skills may need some adjusting.

When you communicate with your spouse, speak and listen respectfully, honestly and with love. Have a forgiving heart so that if they do say something that offends, you can respond with love instead of anger or hurt. Or if they are not giving you the attention you would like, you can talk to them about it. Remember not everyone thinks alike, and *the way the other person is processing your communication* may be the real issue, not your spouse.

Put on then, as God's chosen ones, holy and beloved, compassionate hearts, kindness, humility, meekness, and patience, bearing with one another and, if one has a complaint against another, forgiving each other; as the Lord has forgiven you, so you also must forgive. And above all these put on love, which binds everything together in perfect harmony.

Colossians 3:12-14, ESV

It is important that your communication is developed so that you could both learn each other's communicating styles, learn each other's likes and dislikes, learn the real intentions behind certain types of expressions, and so much more. Again, this is a process. You do not simply master communication because suddenly you are sharing well or listening well. It is a complete package and it is possible to find the needed balance.

This does not mean that there will never be any type of misunderstandings going forward. Most certainly this can mean that you can now have the tools and knowledge to sort through the misunderstandings more efficiently, effectively, and above all more lovingly.

Another area that can be difficult is if you need to exercise correction with your spouse. You must learn that just because something is uncomfortable for you to hear, doesn't mean that you shouldn't hear it. Alternatively, just because something is uncomfortable to say, doesn't mean you shouldn't say it.

> *Therefore encourage one another*
> *and build each other up...*
> **1 Thessalonians 5:11, NIV**

Your spouse is supposed to help build you up. That may mean that they may have wisdom on what you are doing or saying. As long as it is done with love and with the affirmation from the Lord, that is what they are to do. Remember that the Lord may be using your spouse to communicate something life changing and important for your life.

If you give correction, then you must also be able to receive correction. Luis has often shown me areas of my life where I could be better, and vice versa. The key is that you are not looking to change your spouse. You are simply offering some insight into an area you see that may be a struggle for them. Because I am naturally always trying to be the helpful one, the one who teaches, this area was difficult for me. I had to learn to stop correcting him all the time, but I also had to learn to be able to receive correction. This should all be done in love, and again with the affirmation of the Lord. If not, it can backfire and cause contention.

Remember it is not your job to change your spouse. That is the job of the Holy Spirit. While the Holy Spirit can prompt you to speak into the life of your spouse, you have to make sure that the prompting is from the Holy Spirit and not your own hidden agenda. Bear in mind that you must also be willing to receive loving correction from your spouse, because it might be the Lord speaking to you through them.

You can take these steps when looking to *give* correction to your spouse:

- *Pray* - Make sure that the correction you are about to give your spouse is indeed from the Lord. If it is not, it can backfire. Make sure your intentions are not selfish; pray to God to search your heart. (Psalms 139:23)

Do you receive correction well from your spouse? If not, what are ways you can change?

_____
_____
_____
_____
_____
_____
_____
_____
_____
_____
_____
_____
_____
_____

So a church leader must be a man whose life is above reproach...he must be able to teach.

1 Timothy 3:2, NLT

When she (wife) speaks, her words are wise, and she gives instruction with kindness.

Proverbs 31:26, NLT

- *Timing* - Make sure that the timing is right; their acceptance of what you want to share can ultimately depend on when you communicate it. (Ecclesiastes 3:7)
- *Choose* - Make sure that you choose the right words to express yourself. The timing may be right, and your intentions good, but the wrong words can cause conflict. (Ephesians 4:29)
- *Truth* - The main reason you are taking this step is that you love them. Make sure you're honest and loving as you speak truth into their lives. (Ephesians 4:15)

You can take these steps when you *receive* correction from your spouse:

- *Listen* - Take the time to hear your spouse out. Do not be on the defensive. (Proverbs 19:20)
- *Pray* - Pray about what your spouse has shared and get confirmation from the Lord as to how to apply it to your life. (Psalms 139:24)
- *Choose* - Choose to accept the correction graciously. It can lead to gaining wisdom, (Proverbs 15:32, Proverbs 8:33)
- *Thank* - Thank the Lord and then your spouse for their love, and make sure that you acknowledge how they have helped you. There is no shame in this. (Psalms 28:7)

Do you give correction well to your spouse? What are ways you can change?

But the fruit of the Spirit is love, joy, peace, patience, kindness, goodness, faithfulness, gentleness, self-control: against such things there is no law.

Galatians 5:22-23, ESV

If you are practicing your communication with God, when the time comes that the Lord is using your spouse, you will have the ability to detect it. Maybe not right away, but after careful analysis and prayer you will be able to acknowledge that the Lord was using your spouse to help you.

If it should take time and not be something that you notice immediately, make sure to communicate to your spouse your gratitude for the courage it took for them to lovingly show you something you could not see yourself. Communicating this can be encouraging to your spouse, and they would take their role in this part of communication more seriously, to ensure that it is not abused.

In Summary

Communication is an important part of any relationship. Communication with God can help you to be better in so many ways. You can be a better person because God will be communicating ways that you can be better for yourself, your family, your friends, and especially your spouse. As you communicate with God through prayer, worship, and through the Bible, you will grow spiritually and the fruit of the Spirit will manifest itself in you, helping you to treat each other better.

You should be actively exercising communication both with God and with your spouse. Communication is an important foundation that can make all other areas of your marriage better including relationship, resolving conflict, sexual intimacy, decision-making and others areas. Your marriage cannot afford lack of communication. Try every effort to lay this foundation right and not compromise the rest of the structure.

Chapter Two - Discussion Questions

What are some of the ways your husband communicates with you? What can you do to react more positively when your communication style differs from his?

_____

_____

_____

_____

_____

_____

_____

_____

_____

_____

_____

_____

_____

_____

_____

_____

Chapter Two – Take Action!

Compare your answer to the question on page 73, with that of your husband's answer on men's page 73. Identify the ways that you both will initiate and build on your communication skills, to create a stronger foundation for your marriage.

_____

_____

_____

_____

_____

_____

_____

_____

_____

_____

_____

_____

_____

_____

_____

_____

_____

_____

Chapter Three

SPECIALIST

I praise you, for I am fearfully and wonderfully made...
Psalm 139:14, ESV

S o far, the blueprints are drawn and the foundation is laid, and now the real work begins. Each worker has a job to do. In any construction project, it's important that everyone do his or her part well in order for the project to be a success. You are charged with your particular task and no one can do that task other than you.

If you're a specialist within a project, no one can do it better than you can. Everyone else's effort to do your specialty will fall short and the construction project will suffer. You have a very special purpose in your relationship. Your husband cannot do what you're tasked by God to do and you, as a wife and/or mother are not able to do what your husband is tasked by God to do. In this construction project, God is the designer and owner of the project, and you are to follow His orders.

This is one of the two chapters in this book that differs from the men's version. I can be different with how I speak to you because I am speaking directly and only to you as a woman. My husband will speak directly and only to your husband as well. I am going to try my best to be transparent, open, and honest because that is what the Lord has laid upon my heart. It's difficult to identify our true purpose, with all the confusion that comes from modern society. In this chapter we will focus on uncovering what the Bible teaches us is a wife's role.

Woman to Woman

Woman to woman, I can tell you that I understand the challenges we face, and how difficult marriage can be. When I started this study, I talked about how difficult it was for me to adapt, and how I learned God's design and plan for marriage. Then I moved on to how I had to build communication with the Lord and communication with my husband. While what I have shared with you is truly possible, I am not going to pretend that it's easy or quick because it's not. In fact, I learn more every day.

We still argue and we still have issues. By no means am I an expert at marriage. But with over 20 years of marriage to my husband, and facing new challenges as time passes, I have learned many do's and don'ts. I have also learned, that even though times can be difficult, there are many more times that can be beautiful. I have learned to appreciate my husband and our differences. I have learned to love him more than I ever thought I could, and my life is more amazing with him in it. Through all the difficulties, I love him still and want nothing more than to have the marriage God has destined for my life.

Before I could work on my marriage, I had to understand that I needed to focus on making myself better for both God and for my husband. In the first few years, my focus was on Luis. I tried my best to make him into the ideal husband for me. I tried my best to teach him how he should love me, how he should show me he cared, how he should treat me, how I wanted him to treat my family and friends, and how he should act in front of them, etc. I had put in such a tall order for who I thought he needed to be for me, that I failed to realize all that I was *not* for him

Learning to be a Godly Wife

It's hard to admit our flaws and shortcomings, but I had to admit that I was trying to change the wrong person. I needed to start a change in me. We all have different areas that we need to improve in, but I'm going to share with you the steps I've taken to work on my own issues in hopes that this will help you. Be encouraged by knowing that God can help us to be all that we were meant to be, in all areas of our life.

> *And I am certain that God, who began the good work within you, will continue his work until it is finally finished on the day when Christ Jesus returns.*
>
> **Philippians 1:6, NLT**

God is so awesome because He is the one who is doing the work in us. Be encouraged that we're never alone and that our lifelong growing process is going to be according to God's timing, to His will, and for our good. If we think that we're not where we should be, we can be encouraged because God will help us.

First Things First

It's important to reach your full potential as a woman, a wife, a mother, a family member, a friend, a professional, etc. You do many different jobs, and there is nothing wrong with wanting to be great at them all. Your priorities must be in order so that you can achieve your goals in all these areas.

There are many things that you learn throughout your life that can be damaging. There comes a time that you must unlearn those things, and accept the correct things in order to be better.

You need to know what your priorities are. This can get confusing. Some believe that their children should be the number one priority, or their husband, or their jobs, etc. Your number one priority, as a Christian, must be your relationship with God. You make God your first priority through communication, relationship, and obedience. You do this by praying, reading God's Word and finding time to worship Him.

Don't confuse the *church* with *God*. God is who you have a relationship with, and the church is where you go to grow spiritually. Yes, you are to go to church, plug into your church, take time to serve in your church, but in no way does that come before your husband or your family.

Your prayers, Bible devotion, and worship are how you put God first. These will bless the Lord's heart, and you will be immensely blessed in all areas of your life and in your marriage. When you pray and read His Word, you can identify what God has to say about the things you should be doing.

When you place God first, all other things in your life will be supplied to you. God will make sure that you have everything you need, including what you need to improve your marriage. Two very important things you need to do your best as a wife, are discernment and wisdom. Discernment helps you to know when something is right for you and your family. Discernment comes from the Lord, but only through a true relationship with Him.

Is God your number 1 priority? What changes do you need to make to enrich your relationship with the Lord?

Seek the Kingdom of God above all else, and live righteously, and he will give you everything you need.
Matthew 6:33, NLT

And it is my prayer that your love may abound more and more, with knowledge and all discernment.
Philippians 1:9, ESV

As for wisdom, God is so good, that in no way does He expect you to know all the answers. In fact, He tells us to ask Him for the wisdom we need. This includes every area of our life including our marriages. We just need to take out the time to ask. Our lives can get busy, but we must always make time to pray and seek the Lord.

Husbands Next

Your next priority should be your husband. Some may believe it's their children, but that isn't Biblical. The Bible is clear that you are "one flesh" with your spouse.

> *"31 Therefore a man shall leave his father and mother and hold fast to his wife, and the two shall become one flesh." 32 This mystery is profound, and I am saying that it refers to Christ and the church. 33 However, let each one of you love his wife as himself, and let the wife see that she respects her husband.*
> **Ephesians 5:31-33, ESV**

Look closely at these verses. I've already talked about joining with your spouse as one flesh as a reason to show why you were meant to be married, but this is more profound than that. Verse 31 explains not only the joining of two individuals; it also shows how you left your parents to be together.

Have you demonstrated to your husband that he is the main priority in your life? What ways can you show him?

_____

_____

_____

_____

_____

_____

_____

_____

_____

_____

_____

_____

_____

_____

If you need wisdom, ask our generous God, and he will give it to you. He will not rebuke you for asking.

James 1:5, NLT

A wise woman builds her home, but a foolish woman tears it down with her own hands.

Proverbs 14:1, NLT

You are now responsible for each other in a way that is described as profound, and it compares it to Christ and the church. Just like Christ is number one for the church, your husband, after God, should be number one to you. In the same way that you're first to your husband, he should love you as he loves himself.

I know that your love for your children is huge. I have three children of my own, and can completely see how sometimes I want to go up against the world for them.

However, the job of raising your children only lasts a short time. The time will come that they will leave to start their own lives. When this happens, you and your husband are the last ones standing in your home. If you spent your years dedicating your time and effort to your children as your priority, then when it's only the two of you, your relationship will have a void.

The emphasis that God puts on staying in your marriage is an important one, and even the Bible states that it's a profound mystery, meaning something that cannot be understood completely.

Notice the comparison of the relationship between Christ and the church, to the relationship between husband and wife. Also, building your husband up is actually for the benefit of your children because he can be a better father, provider, and friend to them if he is cared for in the way God intended.

How should you treat your husband? What kind of relationship should you have with him? This is where it gets confusing. When you feel as though you aren't a priority, or if you're having some troubles, it's very hard for you to be motivated to be the loving wife that your husband expects. So I will share some of the things I did that changed my marriage in a great way.

First, I had to stop trying to change Luis. I had to focus on changing myself. So how did I do that? I had to surrender my life and everything in me to the Lord. It wasn't easy, but I did it. The process wasn't quick, but it was effective. I started by praying.

After I realized that I couldn't change Luis, I understood who the only one that could was, and that was God. So, I started to pray for Luis every day. I prayed over him for every area in his life. I prayed that he would have wisdom. I prayed that God would have His will and way in the life of Luis. I prayed for his spirituality, I prayed for his desires, for his happiness, for his joy, his safety, and I prayed for his love. I prayed so much and I didn't get tired. Everything and anything that I could think of that was good for him, I prayed. I would wait for him to fall asleep and I would lay my hand on his forehead as he slept and I would pray.

Then I prayed for myself. I prayed that God would change my heart into the heart that He wanted. I prayed that I would make Luis happy; I prayed that I would be the wife he needed. I prayed and prayed. Prayer was the right way to start.

I also had to obey what God had to say. I started practicing His perfect instructions. One of His instructions is:

21. And further, submit to one another out of reverence for Christ. 22. For wives, this means submit to your husbands as to the Lord. 23. For a husband is the head of his wife as Christ is the head of the church. He is the Savior of his body, the church. 24. As the church submits to Christ, so you wives should submit to your husbands in everything.

Ephesians 5:21-24 NLT

There is so much truth in these few verses that, if obeyed, can be marriage changing. Look at verse 21. It states to submit to one another out of reverence for Christ. I know the word submit can be difficult accept. This can be even more difficult if you're an independent woman, because in today's society there is so much emphasis on the sexes being treated equally, without regard to our differences.

The word "submission" has such a negative connotation, that you might overlook that the verse says that *both* of you are to submit to one another. You do this in different capacities, but each out of reverence to Christ. This meaning that you should be submissive at a minimum because of your obedience to the Lord. Therefore, if you don't submit to your husband, then you're directly disobeying God, and bringing shame to God's Word.

Write down some of your thoughts on submission? Is this an area that you can work on?

_____

_____

_____

_____

_____

_____

_____

_____

_____

_____

_____

_____

_____

_____

_____

_____

_____

These older women must train the younger women to love their husbands and their children, to live wisely and be pure, to work in their homes, to do good, and to be submissive to their husbands. Then they will not bring shame on the word of God.

Titus 2:4-5, NLT

What Submission Means - And *Doesn't* Mean

In Ephesians 5, verses 21-24 (page 94) you see what submission means for the wife. You are to submit to your husband because he is the head. God designated it this way and no amount of independence can change God's Word and order. Your husband is the leader in your marriage and the leader of your household. He is responsible for you and your home. When you're not submissive, you strip him away from that responsibility, and he cannot be all that God has designed him to be. Before I go any deeper, let's look at what submission is *not*.

Submission doesn't mean that you're in anyway less valuable than he is. He isn't superior to you. You both have equal value in the eyes of the Lord, you simply have different roles and different purposes.

Just because your husband is named the leader of your home, this doesn't mean that God values him more. You're both one in Christ. In the eyes of the Lord there are no differences in your value, He loves you equally. However, there is a difference in the purpose you serve and in how He has designed you. Nevertheless, each purpose is equally significant, and equally valuable, you're just purposed in your own unique way for the Lord.

There is no longer Jew or Gentile, slave or free, male and female.
For you are all one in Christ Jesus.

Galatians 3:28, NLT

Submission doesn't mean that you no longer have a say or an identity. Your input is still valuable and should be taken into consideration in all decisions. He is the leader who makes the final call, but he should value your input and understand that you're both dependent on each other.

Although you're to be submissive to him, you both have your own identity and are both valuable to each other as individuals. You both have a certain level of dependency on each other. As leaders have a dependency on their team, so does your husband have with you.

Submission doesn't mean that your husband is allowed to abuse you, take advantage of you, or mistreat you in anyway. On the contrary, as the head of his house, your husband is to love you as Christ loved the church. This type of love is sacrificial, and not harming. He is to care for you as he should care for his own body.

Being submissive also doesn't mean that you are to allow your husband to give you a directive that would bring any type of harm to yourself. Anything that can harm you spiritually, physically, socially, mentally, emotionally, or lawfully. This means that he cannot lead you to anything sinful, anything illegal, anything that can be detrimental to your person in any fashion or way, for all of these things violate God's Word.

Submission is sometimes considered taboo. It's such a shame because it's the perfect will of the Lord. As I've explained what submission is not, you can clearly see that submission is actually

But among the Lord's people, women are not independent of men, and men are not independent of women.

1 Corinthians 11:11, NLT

_____

_____

_____

_____

_____

_____

_____

_____

_____

_____

_____

_____

For husbands, this means love your wives, just as Christ loved the church.

Ephesians 5:25, NLT

In the same way, husbands ought to love their wives as they love their own bodies. For a man who loves his wife actually shows love for himself.

Ephesians 5:28, NLT

not a bad thing. Yes, the Lord tells us to submit, but with that submission comes love and protection for us. There is so much that your husband is responsible for, that you can see God's love and care for you, and just how very special you are.

I admit that this was difficult for me to do. I didn't want anyone to be in charge of me, and I knew what was best. I have the strength and the intellect to do all things without a man. However, I found out that I didn't have to, and that surrendering myself to God's plan was actually better. I'm not going to say that I never want to be in charge, but I do know that with obedience to God comes great blessing.

One thing that I have learned from my husband and many other men that I have spoken with is that a man wants our submission. Submission to our husbands means so many things. When you submit, you are yielding to his leadership. You're empowering him to be the head of your person. You're saying to him that you honor him as the leader of your children and your home.

Submission is showing your husband that you love and trust God's Word when it says to follow your husband as the leader. Your submission will demonstrate your respect for him. You want him to feel your trust in his ability to lead, trust in his wisdom and intellect, and trust in his love for you and your family. When you

What are ways that you can show your husband that you honor and respect him?

_____

_____

_____

_____

_____

_____

_____

_____

_____

_____

_____

_____

_____

_____

_____

_____

But there is one thing I want you to know: The head of every man is Christ, the head of woman is man, and the head of Christ is God.

1 Corinthians 11:3, NLT

love completely, you don't lose faith in that person. You are confident that your husband will lead the way God intended.

Even if now they may not be leading the way that you think they should, your encouragement can help him go in the right direction. Some women may think that their husband isn't able for many different reasons; however, that's not your call. It's God's call. You may be utterly wrong in that assessment. He didn't say to only submit if they're capable, He said to submit, plain and simple. God will take care of the rest.

Your obedience to the Lord will unlock the blessing in your marriage that you hope for. This is why the Bible says to do it out of reverence to God. When you submit even though you might not want to, not only are you trusting your husband, but also bigger than that, you're trusting God.

Respect is one of the main things that empowers and encourages your husband in your marriage. When you submit to your husband, you're saying you respect and honor God's authority in your marriage and family. This means that you have to be careful not to have a bad attitude when things aren't the way you expected. A bad attitude is disrespectful, and discouraging.

Make sure that your attitude toward your husband is loving and respectful. This helps your husband to become the husband he is meant to be, the father he is meant to be, and the spiritual man

Love never gives up, never loses faith, is always hopeful, and endures through every circumstance.

1 Corinthians 13:7, NLT

...and the wife must respect her husband.

Ephesians 5:33, NLT

he is meant to be. When you respect and honor your husband, it can help draw him closer to God.

> *1 Wives, respect and obey your husbands in the same way. Then the husbands who do not obey the word of God will want to know God. They will want to know God because their wives live good lives, even though they say nothing about God. 2 They will see that you live holy lives and respect your husbands. 3 You should not be fine on the outside only. Some women make their hair nice. They wear gold things. They have fine clothes 4 But you must be fine in your heart. Have a heart that is gentle and quiet. That will not wear out. And God thinks it is worth very much. 5 There were holy women long ago who trusted in God. They made themselves nice in this way. They obeyed their husbands. 6 Sarah obeyed Abraham. She called him her master. You are her children if you do what is right and are not afraid of trouble.*
> **1 Peter 3:1-6, WE**

Submission means many things. It can be hard, especially when you think things aren't right. But if you live the way that God designed you, your submission can help your husband to be the man God intended; the man that is the best for you.

Submitting to Luis, even when I didn't feel like it, spoke volumes to him. He talks about it all the time. How much he appreciated that I gave him the respect he wanted, even though he felt like he didn't deserve it. He says that my actions motivated him to be better with me. When he saw that I cared enough to do my best, even when he wasn't at his best, he said that it always inspired him to try to be better.

Don't get me wrong, we still and will always have our moments because we are human and make mistakes, or simply because we might be having a bad day. However, we try hard each day to be better to each other. For us women, the Word of God is clear on the power we have to build or break our homes, and so we have lots of responsibility.

You may think that because God designated your husband as the leader that He entrusted your husband with more than He entrusted you, but that is not true. We have so much that God is entrusting in our hands, we just have to be willing to do our best with what God has given.

So, all this talk about submission, but how, specifically, do we do this? There are many things that we can be and can do while submitting to our husbands. The first thing that you must know is that submission and all that it entails is a choice. It's your choice to make. It's in your hands to invest this into your marriage. Remember that when you're submitting you're yielding, loving, trusting, respecting, and honoring your husband.

Your submission goes hand in hand with your words and actions. Your words and actions have lots of power. So, if you're saying you're submitting, but not actually putting it into practice, this is not submission. If you're physically following what he wants but are whining, complaining or criticizing him, then that's not submission either.

You have the power to build up or break down your husband. Your action of submitting, as described in 1 Peter 3:1 (page 104), can not only bring your husband closer to God, but can help him to value you more, and see you more beautifully. However, if you do not submit to your husband, the ramifications can be the total opposite. You can actually drive your husband away from God and away from you. This doesn't mean that if your husband isn't serving the Lord that it's your fault. Please don't confuse what I am saying.

We each have the freewill to choose. If he isn't serving the Lord and you're trying to present the gospel, but aren't obeying the Word, this can cause damage to how he views Christ and the church. But the great thing about the Lord is that He is a Lord of second chances. You can absolutely decide to start today.

Putting it Into Action

So what type of words or actions should you practice? Primarily, you must show love to your husband by accepting who he is. Your love should be unconditional. When you're constantly trying to change him, you give him the feeling that you don't accept him for who he is. This can damage his ego, give him insecurities, and discourage him. He can feel as though you're taking note of his performance or measuring him to some standard. Remember it's the job of the Holy Spirit to change him, not yours.

Accept him with everything that he comes with. Yes, he will fail at some things, but so will you. You both are imperfect, and under construction. Therefore, you must show him that despite the times he fails, you still accept and love him. Human beings can be more forgiving of their own failures and shortcomings than those of others. Open your heart and allow him the freedom to make mistakes, for you sure will make your own mistakes.

Another way to show that you love him is by putting him first. Make sure he can see, feel, and know that he is a priority, that his needs are important to you. There is such a misconception that women want all the attention, but in reality, men want just as much if not sometimes even more. Men want to feel wanted. They want to feel admired, and longed for. They want to know that they are important in your life.

Make sure that you're saying and showing him that you're thankful that he's in your life. This can be a great encouragement to your husband, and shows your loyalty to him and all he is. Shows him how much you appreciate and care for him.

When he feels that you value him as your leader, your advisor, your lover and your friend, his desire to be better will naturally happen, and God will be working in his heart as well.

If you want to demonstrate your submission with love, one other thing that you must do is be a cheerleader. That's right, I said *cheerleader*. You should encourage your husband any way you can. When you submit, you're encouraging him as a leader. But you need to choose your actions and words to do this.

Saying you believe in him, or have faith in his judgment, is always helpful. Don't shame him. Say and show him that you're proud of him; this demonstrates that you admire who he is, and what he does for you and your family.

Give him words of encouragement like, "Great job," or "I'm glad you thought of that," or "You handled that great!" Your husband needs encouragement; he needs your support. There are so many things that he is dealing with on a daily basis. Women juggle many things as well, but love is sacrificial. Your husband is trying to excel while wearing many hats, just as you are.

He wants to be successful in his career, among his friends, and relatives, and especially with you at home. He wants your admiration and respect. Lack of these things can cause pressure.

The enemy can surely attack when these pressures aren't being alleviated in some way at home. Don't add to these pressures. When you do right by him, you build his trust in you.

Find ways to enrich the life of your husband. One of the best ways is to be helpful. Remember you are his helper. God made you as a powerful support for your husband. Again, don't take this as

Think about the last time you told or showed your husband that you were grateful for something he had done. Think about the last time you gave him encouragement. Write about how you can do this more often.

An excellent wife is the crown of her husband, but she who brings shame is like rottenness in his bones.

Proverbs 12:4, ESV

offensive, or believe that being a helper is insignificant. God refers to Himself as *Helper*. The Holy Spirit is referred to as *The Helper*.

How awesome that wives have such a great title, full of worth. God is so good and desires nothing more than for you to be fulfilled in many ways. One of these ways is by being a helper to your husband, helping to build him up and be the man God called him to be.

Help your husband to be all that he can be without trying to control or change him. Offer your assistance when needed. Offer your support and understanding. Help him to stay focused on his responsibilities and priorities.

While each of us is responsible for our own actions and responsibilities, life can throw distractions his way, and sometimes he could be just plain tired, or discouraged. A loving and encouraging help to keep him focused goes a long way.

The Third Priority

Although this book is specifically about marriage, children have a place in the discussion of priorities. After God, and then your spouse, the next priority is your children.

Parenting is difficult enough alone. But you are tasked by God to raise them together, making differences between spouses even more difficult.

Her husband can trust her, and she will greatly enrich his life.
She brings him good, not harm, all the days of her life.
Proverbs 31:10-11, NLT

_____

_____

_____

Be honest; are there ways that you demonstrate admiration for your husband?

_____

_____

_____

What are some ways that you can be helpful to your husband, outside of your normal responsibilities?

_____

_____

_____

Behold, God is my helper; the Lord is the upholder of my life.
Psalm 54:4, ESV

But the Helper, the Holy Spirit, whom the Father will send in my name, he will teach you all things and bring to your remembrance all that I have said to you.
John 14:26, ESV

You both are parents, and you should work together in the raising of your children. A strong partnership is the best way to demonstrate to your children a united vision where you both share authority.

Together you should search for the wisdom God provides to instruct and raise your children. Pray with your husband for wisdom, for your relationship, for your children, and for everything else that is needed for your home.

As a wife and a mother, it's important that you do your best to not only build your husband up, but your children, as well. Nurture them as they discover how to be the persons that God calls them to be.

You both are their first teachers in every aspect of life. As a mom, you can teach them how to love God, how to have relationships, how to communicate, and about kindness, reward, and discipline. Your devotion to God and to your husband will teach your children immensely. You are their first example.

You need to dedicate time to the teaching of your children. It isn't enough just to provide for their physical needs. You are their first guide in the way they should go with their relationship with the Lord, and guiding their character so that they could be the best that they can be. Part of this is to nurture and love, and the other is to instill discipline.

...women to love their husbands and their children.
Titus 2:4, NLT

My child, listen when your father corrects you. Don't neglect your mother's instruction.
Proverbs 1:8, NLT

A house is built by wisdom and becomes strong through good sense. Through knowledge its rooms are filled with all sorts of precious riches and valuables.
Proverbs 24:3-4, NLT

When she speaks, her words are wise, and she gives instructions with kindness.
Proverbs 31:26, NLT

Your child will learn what is right and wrong from you first. They're not only receiving instruction from you, but they are watching what you do, so you need to be the best example possible. This is a big responsibility, but God will give you the wisdom and the strength if you ask for it. Above everything that you can teach, is the love that you and only you can provide, and you will forever be blessed.

When you lean on God's understanding of how to be a good wife and mother, your husband and children will love and respect you for all your efforts. I know that some of these things may not be easy to do immediately, and none of us are perfect. I am still learning each day to be a better wife and mother. I can only continuously seek the Lord in prayer and through His Word.

Your priorities are God, husband, and children, but most women value a good friendship. It's good to get support from your Godly friends.

This doesn't mean that you have to share anything private or specific, but God instructs those that are older and full of wisdom to teach others about these things.

But as for you, teach what accords with sound doctrine.

Titus 2:1, ESV

Direct your children onto the right path, and when they are older they will not leave it.

Proverbs 22:6, NLT

The rod and reproof give wisdom, but a child left to himself brings shame to his mother.

Proverbs 29:15, ESV

Discipline your son, and he will give you rest; he will give delight to your heart.

Proverbs 29:17, ESV

_____

_____

_____

_____

_____

_____

_____

_____

_____

_____

Her children rise up and call her blessed; her husband also, and he praises her: "Many women have done excellently, but you surpass them all." Charm is deceitful, and beauty is vain, but a woman who fears the Lord is to be praised.

Proverbs 31:28-30, ESV

Older women likewise are to be reverent in behavior, not slanderers or slaves to much wine. They are to teach what is good, and so train the young women to love their husbands and children, to be self-controlled, pure, working at home, kind, and submissive to their own husbands, that the word of God may not be reviled.

Titus 2:3-5, ESV

God wants you to learn from wise counsel. You have to choose wisely, and always assuring that you bring no shame to your husband or children when you speak to them.

For the most part, women like to talk and interact with other women. Choose your friendships wisely. If the person is counseling anything that is contrary to what God's Word teaches, then she isn't the right counsel. Seek women that are Holy Spirit filled and led. Take time to relax and share with friends, it's good for your own relief and enjoyment.

In Summary

Your priorities are God, your husband, your children, and then everything else. You are to seek the Lord and His wisdom in order to reach your full potential. Don't focus on changing your husband. That is the job of the Holy Spirit. But you can help your husband by submitting to God's Word, and to God's authority by being submissive to your husband. Your prayer, love, respect, honor, support, encouragement, and help is good for the building up of your husband. Your love, nurturing, teaching, example, discipline, and guidance is needed by your children. Although this sounds like a tall order, God can and will help you to achieve all these things. Godly friendships and counsel can also be helpful and is good for you to build relationships with others for your own personal relief and enjoyment. Women are charged to do much, but if you trust God and His Word, you will never be disappointed.

Chapter Three - Discussion Questions

Are there any areas in your life where you may not be fulfilling your role as a wife? What will you do to improve in these areas? How can your husband help you to improve?

_____

_____

_____

_____

_____

_____

_____

_____

_____

_____

_____

_____

_____

_____

_____

Chapter Three – Take Action!

Compare your answer to the question on page 101, with that of your husband's answer on men's page 115. Decide together which are the most important ways that you each will show your love and respect for the other, and commit to showing your appreciation in these ways.

Chapter 4

TEAMWORK

I appeal to you…
that you be united in the same mind and the same judgment.
1 Corinthians 1:10, ESV

So far we've done some hard work, and you're halfway there. This construction project is working out fine. To recap, the blueprints have been designed, the foundation has been laid, and everyone is operating in their perspective function.

However, a construction job also requires some team effort. There are roles and work that has to be properly executed by each person individually, but there are other things that take more than one person to be able to accomplish. Things that can only be done with teamwork.

In case you haven't realized it yet, you and your spouse are both a team, and must function as one unit. You each have your individual role or function, but teamwork is what's going to make this construction project be successful. It's only through harmonious teamwork that a project is completed.

Teams don't always work in harmony. Troubles come and cause contention between the team. The team must find ways to see past their differences and continue forward with the project. At other times, troubles or obstacles come against the project altogether and the team must make every effort to do their part to save the project and the team members themselves.

Well, this is exactly what happens in your marriage. You get into disagreements, or face issues or problems that cause arguments and strife in your marriage. Or the enemy comes up against your marriage in order to destroy it. The enemy tries his best to ruin your marriage. He hates what your marriage stands for and wants nothing more than to destroy it. He is against your union, and against the harmony and stability of your children and your home.

Conflict Happens

First, you must know that conflict in marriage is absolutely normal. Conflict will always exist because we are all different human beings, with different thoughts, ideas, and opinions. It's not the conflict that defines you. It's how you resolve the conflict that will ultimately speak about who you are in Christ. Sometimes conflict is fairly easy to resolve. At other times, conflict seems like it's impossible to move past. Be encouraged and know that you can do all things through Christ who strengthens you, and this includes resolving conflicts.

There are many types of challenges that cause the conflict that most couples face. Common challenges are finances, work or school schedules, child-rearing, in-laws and friends. Sometimes you'll disagree on where to go, or what to do.

Problems may escalate, depending on how strongly you feel about the issue. Conflict happens when your expectations are not met. One or both of you might feel unappreciated, or undervalued. It's hard to move past disagreements and disappointments. It's especially difficult when you feel that your rights have been violated.

Conflict can be difficult and can add strain, but conflict resolution can cause the conflict to be a blessing in disguise. It can help you to understand each other better and gives you an opportunity to grow. The Word of God speaks to you about how conflict helps increase your faith, but it also helps to mature you. When conflict strikes, try to learn from the experience.

I know that trying to learn from a disagreement is easier said than done, but it is possible to take from your disagreements things that can be positive for your relationship. As you grow together through each conflict, you will learn more about each other. You'll also learn to be a bit more patient each time. Each time a bit more understanding.

What are the areas of your marriage you feel you struggle with the most? What are some ways that you can make improvements?

_____

_____

_____

_____

_____

_____

_____

_____

_____

_____

_____

_____

_____

_____

_____

_____

Consider it pure joy, my brothers and sisters, whenever you face trials of many kinds, because you know that the testing of your faith produces perseverance. Let perseverance finish its work so that you may be mature and complete, not lacking anything.
James 1:2-4, NIV

Who's Your Enemy?

Another important thing that you must know is that your spouse is not your enemy. Your one and only enemy is Satan. You have to make sure that you know and remember this fact when you are in the middle of a conflict. Don't treat your spouse as your enemy; your spouse is certainly not your enemy. It can feel as though as you are sleeping with the enemy at times, but you must know that it's not so. Your true enemy is the Devil, and he will try to bring everything he can to come against you and your spouse.

Sometimes you can get so angry and treat your spouse as though they are your enemy, when in fact, you are told to love your spouse. For men, this love is an unconditional and sacrificial love that is compared to how Christ loves the church, and for women, a love that is compared to how the church loves Christ.

This is a tall order, but it is possible if you keep Christ in the center of your marriage. You must take the steps and actions necessary to love your spouse in the way that God wants us to love. Your marriage is a reflection of the relationship between Christ and the church.

Think about the ways you may have treated your spouse and ask yourself if these are ways that Christ would treat the church, or if these are ways that the church would treat Christ.

Have you ever treated your spouse like your enemy? What are some ways you can avoid this in the future?

_____

_____

_____

_____

_____

_____

_____

_____

_____

_____

_____

_____

_____

_____

For we are not fighting against flesh-and-blood enemies, but against evil rulers and authorities of the unseen world, against mighty powers in this dark world, and against evil spirits in the heavenly places.

Ephesians 6:12, NLT

No one is perfect, but you must strive to live Christ-like. The first person after God that you should be striving to love unconditionally is your spouse.

Why Conflict?

Conflict occurs because people all have different thoughts and ideas. A conflict can also occur because of your desires. The first conflict occurred in the Garden of Eden. The serpent tempted Eve, and the fruit became desirable to her. Through that desire, she reached out and ate it. When Adam also ate the fruit, they came to understand about good and evil, and they were no longer living in innocence. Sin entered the world. Sin causes the communication lines to be broken between man and woman, and between all of us and God.

There were consequences because of the sin that was committed in the Garden of Eden, and these consequences cause conflict. There is conflict between Satan and man. God, at that moment, did provide a solution with the promise of Christ when He said that the seed of the woman would crush Satan's head. Nonetheless, there is conflict.

Sin is the root cause of all conflict. Some may say desire, but Eve's desire is not what caused their eyes to be opened. Their eyes were opened only after they ate, not after they desired. The desire or temptation will come, but it is what you do when it does come

Think back to your first conflict together. Do you feel you have grown since then? How?

_____

_____

_____

_____

_____

_____

_____

_____

_____

_____

_____

The woman was convinced. She saw that the tree was beautiful and its fruit looked delicious, and she wanted the wisdom it would give her. So she took some of the fruit and ate it. Then she gave some to her husband, who was with her, and he ate it, too. At that moment their eyes were opened, and they suddenly felt shame at their nakedness. So they sewed fig leaves together to cover themselves.

Genesis 3:6-7, NLT

I will put enmity between you and the woman, and between your offspring and her offspring; he shall bruise your head, and you shall bruise his heel.

Genesis 3:15, ESV

that matters. When you desire something specific and it is not provided, this can cause emotions to rise. It can cause anger, disappointment, or hurt.

There is nothing wrong with emotion, but sometimes the actions you take because of an emotional feeling can be wrong. Anger is a normal feeling. You get angry when you feel that your spouse has violated your rights, your needs, and your self-worth. It is not wrong to get angry, but you must be careful of your actions when you do get angry. You can't allow yourself to be ruled by your anger, because this can lead to sin.

Anger is a very strong emotion. It can serve in positive ways. You can use anger as a motivation to get things resolved or do things better. For example, you can be angry that something was not completed, and then you decide to complete it.

Anger can also lead to things that can harm you or your relationship. Out of anger, you can do or say harmful things to your spouse. Anger can cause you to house bitterness in your heart, or in the heart of your spouse. Anger can lead to depression, resentfulness, isolation, and other things that can cause not only conflict in your marriage, but also put a strain on your communication and relationship with each other, and more importantly, your communication and relationship with God.

Let's look at the definition of conflict. Conflict is a serious disagreement or argument. It doesn't always *start* with something serious. Sometimes conflict starts out with the silliest or the most

Do you let your anger get the best of you? What are some things you need to change to avoid this anger?

_____

_____

_____

_____

_____

_____

_____

_____

_____

_____

_____

_____

What causes quarrels and what causes fights among you? Is it not this, that your passions are at war within you? You desire and do not have, so you murder. You covet and cannot obtain, so you fight and quarrel. You do not have, because you do not ask.

James 4:1-2, ESV

And "don't sin by letting anger control you…

Ephesians 4:26, NLT

insignificant things, and then escalates to something bigger, and before you know it, is has blown out of proportion. This can occur when there is stress from other issues, or when you keep things inside and don't communicate them. Then when something comes up that is small, it escalates into something else.

In a previous chapter, I have shared with you some of my thoughts on what it takes to develop your relationship and communication with God, and then each other. You can use some of these thoughts to be better at resolving conflict.

Your relationship and communication with God will help you to be wiser about the things you need to resolve with each other. Better communication and relationship with each other will also help for a much smoother resolution process when conflict occurs. There are other things that you must be ready to do, and ready to accomplish in your relationship if you want to bring conflict resolution into your marriage in a better way.

Confronting

So far, communication has been a key topic throughout these sessions, and it is no different here. Communication is the foundation. I shared with you about how each of us has a different communication style. Sometimes, because of the different styles, and the lack of the understanding of these different styles, your spouse may be offended, which can cause hurt, pain or anger. Even if you know the communication style of your spouse, sometimes they can still end up offended. Luis and I have suffered many times in our own marriage because of this very thing.

I know what he means, but I still can't help feeling hurt or angry when he expresses himself in a certain way, and vice-versa. This is mainly because we're emotional beings.

Some people are more emotional than others are, but none of us are robots, and we don't analytically compute every detail. Some days you can shrug it off and keep moving, and some days you just feel like you can't deal with it. This is absolutely normal, because human beings are imperfect. You must choose to make the appropriate responses to your spouse in order to avoid this as much as possible. Try your best to be understanding and patient.

But sometimes this is just not enough. Sometimes you have to communicate your feelings and what he or she is doing that is causing you pain, hurt, or anger.

You have to confront your spouse with what you believe they have done against you. The Lord knew that there would be some difficulty in marriage, and He provides the solution.

Matthew 18:15 (page 133) says to confront the other person, but then it also adds, "If the person listens and confesses it, you have won that person back". This is important because this shows that there is a dynamic to this. If you are the confronter, you must be open and honest, but if you are the offender, you must be willing to listen, and confess. In other words, accept or take responsibility for what you have said or done that has caused the offense.

This could be difficult because you may feel that you're not guilty of what you are being confronted with. However, perception is key. Remember that people have different communication styles, and at times, certain communication styles can be misunderstood. Therefore, it's important to listen to how the other person feels, and accept that you may have provoked that feeling. Even if it was unintentional, you should accept and apologize for it.

Confronting should be done in love. You should speak truthfully and honestly but choose your words carefully. You should not look to accuse your spouse. Remember that perception can be at play. You might assume that your spouse meant to offend or harm you; however, it may not be so. You will need to ensure that you do your best at not offending your spouse when you choose to confront them.

When you confront your spouse, not only do you have to do it in love, but also you have to do it respectfully. Your goal should not be to let them know how bad they did, but to help them to be better. To edify, encourage, and help them.

You may be confronting them because they've hurt you, but your goal should not be to hurt them back. You need to make sure that you're not doing this with an underlying motive. Be sure that you are solely doing it to resolve the conflict and to help build up your spouse.

If you have ever confronted your spouse, was it always in love? List anything you may change in how you do this in the future.

If another believer sins against you, go privately and point out the offense. If the other person listens and confesses it, you have won that person back.

Matthew 18:15, NLT

There may be times that your spouse may have actually meant to hurt or offend you. Consider why this is the case. Usually when a person chooses to do this, it's because they have been hurt or offended. Even if they are purposely doing this, when you confront your spouse, remain calm and express yourself respectfully and in love. One thing I learned from my aunt and now always say is, "when there is a fire, water can put it out." You both can't be fire, when one is fire, then the other should take the role of water.

There are those who don't like to confront their spouse. They keep things that bother them to themselves. This is not good at all. You may think that you are helping the situation because you don't want to cause an argument, or offend your spouse. In fact, you are not only doing harm to yourself; you are also doing an injustice to your spouse. Keeping things bottled up can cause emotional and physical harm to yourself.

When you don't resolve the problem, you don't move beyond it. This can lead to you exploding with anger when your bottle is full to the brim. It can lead to isolation, which interferes with your communication and relationship.

The injustice to your spouse is that you could be holding this offense against them, and without giving them an opportunity to know what they are doing, or even make it right so that they do not continue to do it. When they are unaware that something they are doing is bothering you, you cannot hold them solely responsible for every time they do it again.

Do you take correction well? Are you open to your spouse pointing out ways to improve? How can you be more receiving and understanding?

_____

_____

_____

_____

_____

_____

_____

_____

_____

_____

_____

Instead, we will speak the truth in love, growing in every way more and more like Christ, who is the head of his body, the church.

Ephesians 4:15, NLT

Don't use foul or abusive language. Let everything you say be good and helpful, so that your words will be an encouragement to those who hear them.

Ephesians 4:29, NLT

There are times that you feel that you shouldn't have to confront your spouse because they should know already. Or because it is not your responsibility to point out their flaws. Or they don't deserve for you to make peace with them. You feel that they are the ones at fault, and so you deserve for them to come to you and apologize. I understand this feeling all too well. In fact, there were times when I would sit and argue with God about how I hated to have to be the one making peace, and how it wasn't fair, and that Luis should be the one to come to me.

There were two things I had to learn from these feelings. First, Jesus made himself clear when He said that if you are offended you should go to your brother and point out his fault. He didn't say to wait for the other person to come and make it right with you. Know that confronting your spouse is an act of obedience.

The second thing I had to learn was that my complaining to God about how Luis should be the one coming to me was prideful. Pride is such an ugly thing. Although I would eventually be the one to make peace, deep down inside I felt that it should have been him. I had to put those feelings to the side, and I had to swallow my pride.

God does not want pride within us. When Christ tells us to confront our offender and point out their flaws, not only is He telling us to do this so that we would have peace, but He is telling us to do this so that we can avoid being prideful, or to hold bitterness, anger and other feelings in our hearts.

Do you effectively communicate how you feel? List ways you can improve your communication with your spouse.

Get rid of all bitterness, rage, anger, harsh words, and slander, as well as all types of evil behavior. Instead, be kind to each other, tenderhearted, forgiving one another, just as God through Christ has forgiven you.

Ephesians 4:31-32, NLT

Sometimes pride may lead you to blame your spouse, while at the same time rationalizing away your own flaws and justifying your actions based on their actions. This is the same blame game that Adam and Eve did when they first committed sin, and mankind has been doing it ever since. It is a defense mechanism. But in order for you to work through conflict and be forgiving toward your spouse, you need to do less of pointing fingers and expecting them to change. Instead, do more self-reflection, and start by changing yourself.

One of the ways a marriage is going to be able to be strengthened through conflict, is if each individual takes responsibility to make needed improvements in themselves. You shouldn't try to change your spouse; you should only try to change yourself. Work on yourself, your own flaws, your own attitudes, your own weaknesses, not your spouse's. Your focus needs to be on all the wonderful, positive, and great things about your spouse. It might help to go back to the moment you first fell in love. It's up to you to forgive, and bring peace to your marriage.

Forgiveness

God wants to get rid of all bitterness, rage, and anger because it is not good for you. These feelings, although not sinful, can lead you to do sinful things. They can also lead you to house bitter feelings in your heart. You cannot operate properly with these

Do you act out of anger or pride? What are ways you can improve in this area?

_____
_____
_____
_____
_____
_____
_____
_____
_____
_____
_____
_____
_____
_____
_____
_____

Then Peter came to him and asked, "Lord, how often should I forgive someone who sins against me? Seven times?" "No, not seven times," Jesus replied, "but seventy times seven!"
Matthew 18:21-22, NLT

feelings trapped inside. When Christ tells you to settle these faults with your spouse, He is doing it for your own good.

Instead, God wants you to be kind, tenderhearted and forgiving to one another, just as He forgave you. You didn't deserve forgiveness and yet Christ forgives you for your sins. If you receive forgiveness from the Lord, you should forgive your spouse. It can feel quite tiresome at times when you continuously have to forgive them for the same thing. Maybe it's an area they struggle with like a bad habit, or something that was taught to them growing up. Patience is needed, and forgiveness is a blessing for you both. God forgives you and continues forgiving you daily.

Your forgiveness toward each other should not be conditional. It's not easy, and in fact, it can be very difficult at times, depending on the offense. You must seek the Lord and His guidance when you are having difficulty forgiving your spouse's offense. This does not give your spouse permission to offend you repeatedly. Each of you must strive to be better and not commit the offense again, especially after you have been advised of how the offense is harmful. However, when we forgive, we are demonstrating love.

Sometimes we may feel that forgiving a certain offense is impossible. However, this is not true. Love covers many things. Again, this doesn't mean that it's easy, but it also doesn't mean that it's impossible. You have to seek the Lord and He will help you to forgive.

Choose to forgive. Once you choose to obey the Lord by forgiving, ask Him to help you forgive. Forgiveness is not an instant cure for the hurt, but it is the first step in that direction. God wants us to be free of all the hurt, and He offers forgiveness as a path to that freedom. The path to healing starts with forgiveness. You have to choose and take the right steps and actions to demonstrate that you truly have forgiven. It is not simply by words, but by your actions that you are going to show your forgiveness toward your spouse.

When granting forgiveness, make sure that you specifically state why you are forgiving them. Don't speak in generalities, which can cause your spouse to feel as though you have not truly forgiven them. If you're unclear, they may assume that you have only forgiven him or her for some of the things and not all.

When forgiving your spouse you should also accept any fault of your own in the situation. While they may have been the aggressor, you may have had a hand in provoking that aggression, whether you meant to or not. Being transparent and owning up to your own flaws can help your spouse not only to accept what you are saying, but also be thankful that you pointed out the flaw.

Lastly, when granting forgiveness make sure that you don't hold on to the offense. The idea is to forgive and move on. You may not be able to forget immediately, but that should be between you and God. Don't constantly bring up an offense that you have already forgiven. This can be harmful and strain your relationship.

When you commit to always forgiving each other, it becomes easier to ask for forgiveness before it gets to the point of discussion. Try not to wait for your spouse to come to you with their hurt. If you know that you acted or spoke to them in harmful ways, then own up to what you have done, and ask for forgiveness.

This is so important to God, that He would rather you not go to Him in worship until you have reconciled with your spouse. This also shows your spouse how much you love them, and how much you are truly sorry.

Don't hold back from asking for forgiveness when you need to. The enemy can cause guilt to bring shame and condemnation to yourself due to a way you have acted or things you may have said to your spouse. Don't let the enemy take hold of situations that can be settled with simple communication. Guilt can lead to bitterness and resentment.

Asking for forgiveness can be helpful for you and definitely for your spouse. It can provoke in your spouse the thought of your consideration, responsibility, and commitment to the relationship. Not that it would guarantee that the forgiveness would be immediate, but if you take the first step, it can help in a big way for the healing process.

When you ask for forgiveness make sure you specifically state why you need to be forgiven. A transparent confession is always best. Admitting what you have said or done is important for

Are you holding things against your spouse? What are some things you can offer your spouse forgiveness for?

_____

_____

_____

_____

_____

_____

_____

_____

_____

_____

_____

_____

_____

_____

Most important of all, continue to show deep love for each other, for love covers a multitude of sins.

1 Peter 4:8, NLT

bearing with one another and, if one has a complaint against another, forgiving each other; as the Lord has forgiven you, so you also must forgive.

Colossians 3:13, ESV

healing to begin. When you ask for forgiveness in general, you may not be actually receiving forgiveness for something specifically and that offense can still linger.

Make sure that you are sincere with your apology. Be sincerely remorseful for what you have said or done. More hurt can be caused if your spouse feels that you are not sincere. Also, saying the actual words, "Would you forgive me?" is very powerful. This can open the doors to healing as well.

Remember to forgive yourself. If you have done all you can to ask for forgiveness, make sure that you forgive yourself. The enemy wants to hold you down with feelings of regret and condemnation. God forgave you, your spouse forgave you, and then it's time for *you* to forgive you.

Finally, know when to choose your battles. Be careful not to correct your spouse for every assumed offense. Pause before you react too quickly, to ensure that you fully understand the situation. We need to make sure that we are seeking the Lord's direction in these things before reacting.

There is wisdom in refraining from speaking sometimes. Remember that you and your spouse are a team, and sometimes it is fitting to take one for the team. If you know that what was done to you is not always done and you are sure that it was only because of stress or the circumstance, then keep it. Take one for the team.

Pointing our someone's flaws all the time can be harmful. Women are stereotypically considered to be nagging, but husbands

Are you aware of ways that you may have offended your spouse? What are some things you feel you may need forgiveness for?

So if you are offering your gift at the altar and there remember that your brother has something against you, leave your gift there before the altar and go. First be reconciled to your brother, and then come and offer your gift.

Matthew 5:23-24, ESV

can also be quarrelsome. Make sure that you are not pointing out someone's flaws just because you can. Seek the Lord before you do. To confront or not to confront, that is the question. Well, the answer is, ask the Lord. Always seek the Lord before you confront.

In Summary

Conflict is a difficult area and there isn't a way to avoid it. However, through conflict and its resolution, we can become closer in our relationship if we choose to learn from what we have experienced. Out of love for your spouse, make sure that you keep the lines of communication open so that conflict resolution can occur. Make sure that you both are communicating your hurts, and your apologies to each other. Pray for one another, love and respect one another, and through it all, always seek the Lord's guidance.

Have you given your spouse a hard time with something in particular? Is there an area your spouse struggles with that you can offer more kindness instead of pointing out his or her flaws constantly?

When words are many, transgression is not lacking, but whoever restrains his lips is prudent.

Proverbs 10:19, ESV

Better to live in a desert than with a quarrelsome and nagging wife.

Proverbs 21:19, NIV

Chapter Four - Discussion Questions

How do you communicate to your husband that he has hurt you? Are there ways that you can respond more positively?

_____

_____

_____

_____

_____

_____

_____

_____

_____

_____

_____

_____

_____

_____

_____

_____

_____

Chapter Four – Take Action!

Talk to your husband about something that has been troubling you. Listen as your husband tells you about something that is troubling him. Don't be defensive or unwilling to listen. Ask for or grant forgiveness, if needed. Determine together how you both can improve in these areas.

Chapter 5

DÉCOR

...love the Lord your God with all your heart..,
...Love your neighbor as yourself...
Mark 12:30-32, NLT

You're getting closer to finishing the construction project. Right about now, the project is looking pretty good, but there is still some work to do. All the actual building is out of the way and it is time for some finishing touches. Once the structure of a new building is up the fun part begins. You are working as a team to get to some of the fine details. It's time to decorate the interior. This is the moment to take some thought and time to make everything look and feel just right. Choose all the details that will go into every room, and make sure that it looks fabulous.

In our intimate relationships, it should be the same way, and in this building project, you have two focus points to decorate. Every chapter so far has stressed the importance of your relationship with

God. Always put God first, and when you do, everything else will be successful. Christ should be in the center of your marriage, and on the topic of intimacy, it is no different.

Once again, my husband will be speaking directly to your husband, and for this chapter it will be just us women. Because this topic covers sex, it can be a bit controversial. Some may not be comfortable talking about sexual intimacy, but nonetheless it is an important part of your marriage so to leave it out would be a big mistake.

Intimacy With God

There are different sides of intimacy. There is spiritual intimacy, and physical intimacy. With God, you have spiritual intimacy. Previous chapters discussed prayer, seeking God through His Word, seeking His direction for your marriage, and understanding His plan and purpose for you in your marriage.

Understand that God also has a purpose for you beyond being a wife and mother, which is a more basic purpose as a woman, as His daughter. He loves you individually, and He loves you beyond your comprehension. He knew you before He formed you in your mother's womb (Jeremiah 1:5), and you are fearfully and wonderfully made (Psalms 139:14). Sometimes our personal insecurities get in the way of our relationship with our husband.

We can't understand our true value until we understand just how valuable we are to the Lord. It's most important to establish an intimate relationship with God so that we fully understand His love for us. Chapter 2 shows the sacrifice that Christ made while we were sinners, but there's much more. Christ made that sacrifice for mankind, but what is so awesome is that it wasn't just a general sacrifice. When Christ sacrificed His life, He made the sacrifice specifically thinking of you, your individual being. When you were created in the womb of your mother, He chose each and every one of your attributes. You were meant to be exactly who you are, and He has handpicked you for wonderful things.

You are the daughter of a King. But I want to stress the word daughter, because daughter implies that you have a Father. There are three times in the Bible that the term Abba Father is used (Romans 8:15, Galatians 4:6, and Mark 14:36). This term is important because the word Abba is followed by the word Father. It is important because the word Abba is an Aramaic word that translates to Daddy, but this word is so profound that there is really no English equivalent. As it currently translates, it says Daddy, Father. But, that really isn't what is meant. The word Abba describes a close and intimate relationship that we can have with our Father in heaven. It describes a close intimate relationship between a father and his child, so much so that we can put all our trust - in fact, a child-like trust - in our Father in Heaven.

The love of a Father that is so profound and so deep that it cannot even be translated into a single word. This is important for your marriage, because in order for you to love your husband and be free with him intimately, you have to first love yourself. In order to love yourself, you have to understand just how important, beautiful, and special you really are to the Lord.

The way we do this is by seeking the Lord intimately. When you pray daily, you praise God in your prayer, pray for protection over your family, for the Lord to bless your family, for direction, and you may even pray to feel the spiritual presence from the Lord and receive it. However, there are times that your prayer can get just a bit deeper, where you don't only pray what you know you should pray for, but when you open yourself up unlike your normal daily prayer.

These are the prayers when you let loose and tell God about all the things that bother you, about all the things that you are holding inside and never really let it out. You may think these things, and know that God knows your heart, but I am talking about sitting in a quiet space and acting like God is a person right beside you, hanging on to your every word. This is when you give every part of yourself to God. These are the times that you hold on to God and don't want to let up, just like when Jacob wrestled with the Angel, that he didn't want to let go until he was blessed.

These are the times when you are even the most honest with yourself. It is in those intimate times of prayer that we are able to allow the Lord to rid us of all those insecurities that we have. In those intimate times with the Lord, we are able to feel God's love ever so real, and present. We can feel it, just as much as we can feel an actual touch from another individual. Our spiritual intimacy with God helps us in all other areas of our life, especially when we're intimate with our husbands.

When we engage in intimate relations with our husbands, we are revealing our most private side. We are revealing everything about us. He sees a side to us that no one else sees. We trust our husbands with our most intimate feelings.

Sometimes it is hard to do this openly and without reserve. Our intimate relationship with our husbands will suffer if we lack feelings of self-worth, or have insecurities that we haven't dealt with. The only one that can help cure those things is the Lord. The Lord can heal you through many different ways. Either through a personal encounter with Him, or He could guide you into getting great counsel. However, you must always seek the direction of the Lord for these things.

I am not saying that it will happen overnight, or that it is easy, but you can choose to begin the process of letting go of your insecurities. Intimate time with the Lord is the place to start. The Lord may lead you to seek professional help as well, but the Lord will definitely help you every step of the way, if you allow Him to.

I believed lies of the enemy, and those lies became insecurities. I've grown to believe instead what the Word tells me about myself – that I am fearfully and wonderfully made (Psalm 139:14). I asked the Lord to help me to release all my insecurities.

Allow God to work within you, and allow God to cleanse and heal you of all those things that are standing in the way of not only having a full and abundant relationship with your husband, but for you personally to be freed of these things for good.

Intimacy With Your Husband

God meant for you to have a great intimate relationship with your husband. God intended for you and your husband to have a deeper connection than you can have with any other human being. God gave sex to mankind for a number of reasons. He gave it in order to establish unity between the man and woman, and for procreation. God blessed the union of Adam and Eve, and within the confines of marriage, God wants us to have a pleasurable sexual relationship.

How do you know this? First, because right after He was done with the creation and gave the command to Adam and Eve to be fruitful and multiply, God called everything that He had designed "good," and that includes sex. Sex was meant for good. It is only through the wickedness of mankind, and by the help of the devil, that sex can be twisted into something sinful and ugly. However, through the confines of marriage, which is what God intended, sex is good and beautiful.

Sex is meant to be explored only within your marriage; all else is sexual immorality. In order for your sexual relationship to be satisfying, you and your husband have to have a satisfying relationship in all other areas. This is why the stages of the construction project, which includes blueprint, foundation, individual roles, and working as a team, should all come prior to the interior decorating phase. Those other phases must be worked through first, in order for this stage to be fully attainable. We can't decorate a building that is not built properly.

Men and women are very different when it comes to sexual intimacy. Men approach sex from a more physical viewpoint, more compartmentalized. This means that they have the ability to section off other things that are concerning or affecting them and get right down to business. Women are relational and inclusive, meaning that they need to establish relationship, and that all the things that happen to them during the day, they bring it into the bed.

Another difference is that men are stimulated quickly through sight, smells, and sexual actions. Men concentrate on the act of sex and the feel of the body. Women are stimulated through words, sensual touches, loving attitude, and can only concentrate on the act if she feels these things from her husband.

A man needs to feel desired, respected, and physically wanted or needed. A woman needs to feel security, a sense of intimacy, and emotionally needed. A man is excited quickly, while a woman can take some time. A man is focused, while a woman can be

Are some unresolved issues distracting you from your sexual relationship with your husband? What are those issues?

_____

_____

_____

_____

_____

_____

_____

_____

_____

_____

_____

_____

_____

_____

_____

_____

_____

Now regarding the questions you asked in your letter. Yes, it is good to abstain from sexual relations. But because there is so much sexual immorality, each man should have his own wife, and each woman should have her own husband.

1 Corinthians 7:1-2, NLT

easily distracted. For a man the act is more physical, while for a woman the act is more emotional.

Although these are differences between the man and the woman, a pleasurable and healthy sex-life is attainable. There are times of highs and lows like in any other area, but if you work on the other areas of your marriage, it is possible to have great sexual intimacy. Remember God intended sex to be good for marriage.

Another way we can know that God intended sex to be good is the book Song of Solomon. Song of Solomon holds nothing back and speaks directly about companionship, commitment, passion, love and sex. This book is there to help inspire married couples and their intimate relationships. God has all the answers we need in His Word, including the topic of sex.

In this book, the young woman talks about her relationship with her beloved. We are going to look at how she describes him throughout the book as an example of what our husbands need from us as well. She describes him as her friend, showing that their relationship goes deeper than just physical, but that there is a deeper connection, a true companionship with each other.

We talked about building communication and relationship. Your companionship with each other is important to have a strong and satisfying sexual relationship. Companionship is developed through communication, romance, and non-sexual affection. Make sure that you're spending time together, that you're devoting time specifically to your husband. This becomes harder with children,

Are you giving your husband the companionship he needs?

...Such, O women of Jerusalem,
is my lover, my friend.

Song of Solomon 5:16, NLT

or when careers demand so much time, or when church responsibilities stack up, but it is very important for both of you.

I remember a time when all we did was worry about the kids. We only went out with the kids, we never did anything for ourselves and this put a strain on our relationship. I was so concerned about the well-being of the kids, that I overlooked the well-being of my husband.

Fortunately, my husband made sure to be vocal about this. Had he not been, I might have damaged our relationship if I kept on this path. I recall a friend taking it as a bad thing when her husband said the same thing to her. She expressed how he shouldn't be selfish, and ultimately their relationship suffered for it. You don't need to be fanatical about the upbringing of your children. There is a time for everything, and you need to make time for your husband alone and without your children.

Your sexual relationship can suffer if your companionship with one another is weak. Sometimes you may wonder why your husband doesn't want to communicate with you, or demonstrate an interest in your companionship. It may be a simple problem that you are not giving him the attention and alone time he needs.

The young woman in Song of Solomon also describes her love for him as an everlasting love, a love that she wants to be sealed, a commitment until death. You may think that women are the only ones who want commitment, and want their husbands to demonstrate their love and commitment, but this is also true for

Do you show your husband that your intimate time together is important to you as well? In what ways can you do this?

Place me like a seal over your heart, like a seal on your arm. For love is as strong as death, its jealousy as enduring as the grave...
Song of Solomon 8:6, NLT

men. Your husband wants you to tell him and show him your commitment to him, just as much. I learned this years ago. My husband and I went to a marriage conference, and we had to take time to talk, and he made it clear that he felt as though I wasn't really committed to him.

I was shocked. I thought that only women cared about those things. I had no idea that he also cared about my demonstrated commitment. I thought that my work in the household and my support of him were enough, but I learned that it wasn't. I learned that not only did I have to show him through my work in the home, I had to show him in other ways as well. He wanted to see me interested in the things that bothered him. He wanted to see that I was passionate about him and was there to console him.

Passion is important as well. The young woman describes her passion for him. She talks about how she slept, but her heart was still awake for him. Passion helps keep your sexual relationship from becoming routine.

Try to be fun and spontaneous when you're with your husband. Plan new things that you both love, or even things that he only loves. When doing something different for him, be giving and unselfish. I've been married for over 20 years, and after being married for so long, you can find yourself in a routine. Don't let passion run dry. Make sure that your excitement for your husband is demonstrated to him continuously.

In what ways could you demonstrate your relational commitment to your husband?

_____

_____

_____

_____

_____

_____

_____

_____

_____

_____

_____

_____

_____

_____

_____

_____

_____

I slept, but my heart was awake, when I heard my lover knocking and calling: "Open to me, my treasure, my darling, my dove, my perfect one.

Song of Solomon 5:2, NLT

I will never forget how I planned an outing for us. It was simple. We went to a concert to see his favorite artist. Afterward, we went to a restaurant that he had talked about for years. I made sure that we went to do some of his favorite things. He was totally surprised. My husband saw that I tried my best to make it all about him. He was so grateful that he tried his best to demonstrate all those things right back to me. He then made a real effort to do many things for me at home to make me feel appreciated. This just inspired me to be even more giving, and it kept on going.

The young woman in Song of Solomon also describes and compliments her beloved's physical features, and she talks about her longing for him. This is important to note because we as women are romantic individuals. We like to be romanced, and like our husbands to be very detailed when he is planning a romantic night for us. In addition, although men may not need all the details we long for, they do sometimes need us to show just how much we want them.

It can feel a bit uncomfortable to describe how much you desire your husband, but he needs to hear it just as much as you need to hear it from him. He needs to know that you desire him sexually and that you find him attractive. Think about how much you like to hear from your husband just how beautiful you are.

Sometimes we feel embarrassed to express these types of feelings to our husbands because of how sexual freedom is looked at in women. However, we need to remember that in the confines

Have you vocalized your admiration and interest? What are some things you believe that your husband would like you to say to him?

_____

_____

_____

_____

_____

_____

_____

_____

_____

_____

_____

_____

_____

_____

One night as I lay in bed, I yearned for my lover. I yearned for him, but he did not come.

Song of Solomon 3:1, NLT

My lover is dark and dazzling, better than ten thousand others!

Song of Solomon 5:10, NLT

of our bedroom, we can be open and sexual with our husbands. We need to demonstrate to our husbands that they are pleasing us. He wants to see that you enjoy yourself and are being pleased with him intimately.

Part of your husband's manhood is wrapped up in his sexual ability to please you. This includes his appearance, your desire for him, and your sexual enjoyment. If he doesn't feel that he is pleasing you, or performing well in that area you can damage his ego and his manhood. This leaves room for the enemy to come in and try to tempt your husband.

Another way that you leave room for the enemy to come in and tempt your husband is through refraining from a sexual relationship with him. It is not good to do this to your husband.

Faithfulness is definitely key in your marriage and in your sexual relationship. Unfaithfulness can harm intimacy and trust between the couple. Satan seeks to destroy your marriage, and one way he puts his foot in the door is when we leave a crack open, such as not engaging in sexual relationship with our husband.

Not that it is an excuse for your husband to be unfaithful, but you should not be contributing to his temptation by withholding sex for long periods of time, unless it is due to medical or spiritual reasons such as mutual and agreed upon fasting as shown in the verses found in 1 Corinthians 7:3-5 (page 167).

Think of things that you may need to express to your husband about your sexual relationship.

_____

_____

_____

_____

_____

_____

_____

_____

_____

_____

_____

_____

_____

_____

The husband should fulfill his wife's sexual needs, and the wife should fulfill her husband's needs. The wife gives authority over her body to her husband, and the husband gives authority over his body to his wife. Do not deprive each other of sexual relations, unless you both agree to refrain from sexual intimacy for a limited time so you can give yourselves more completely to prayer. Afterward, you should come together again so that Satan won't be able to tempt you because of your lack of self-control.

1 Corinthians 7:3-5, NLT

If unfaithfulness has been a struggle in your marriage, seek help from the Lord to forgive him, or yourself. The Lord will guide and provide you with the help you need. This may include seeking Godly counsel, or a family therapist. However, I would strongly suggest that you seek the Lord's direction with whom you choose.

You shouldn't use sex as a weapon, a favor, or only have sexual relations as a prize for a good deed. These types of attitudes can harm not only your sexual relationship, but it can harm other areas of your marriage. This can also provoke temptation in your husband to seek the yearning and longing of another woman.

If you are withholding because there is a problem or your sexual relationship is not going well, this is when you need to find the root cause. When your sexual relationship is not going well, it is usually because there is another underlying reason other than the actual act of sex.

Women tend to be more dependent on their inner feelings than men are. Your pleasure in sex is mental, while for men, not so much. It doesn't mean not at all, but for a woman it can be harder to enjoy an intimate encounter if your feelings about other things are not right. This is why communication with each other is important. It is important that you feel comfortable to talk about everything in your marriage, including sex.

If the issue is the actual act, then you will need to be upfront about that as well. However, because feelings can be hurt, and his ego can be damaged, I strongly suggest that you seek the Lord in prayer concerning how you will go about it.

Maybe you do not say something directly, but suggest some things you may want to do in order to do something different or fun within your relationship. There are ways that you can help him to understand what your needs are without hurting his feelings.

Still, you should feel free to express what you like, and what you dislike. You should feel free to discuss what you are comfortable doing and what you are not comfortable doing. You should also be free explore new things with each other and look to please one another. This should all be done within your comfort.

Again, if there is some hesitation on your part, you can definitely pray about it. You can most definitely feel free to talk to God about some of your insecurities first, so that it will be easier when you talk to your husband.

There are other reasons for sexual problems in your relationship. Physical, emotional, mental, or spiritual issues can get in the way of a fulfilled sex life. Physical issues could be due to an actual medical condition.

For example, it's not uncommon for men to experience erectile dysfunction, and these are times that we women should be as understanding as possible. If this is an issue, you must seek medical attention, as it could be an indicator of serious illness, such as heart and vascular disease. This can be difficult to address, but again if your communication lines are open it can be easier to discuss. Through prayer and understanding, and some medical advice, as needed, you can get through this time.

Sometimes the physical issue is simply fatigue. Whether it is you or your husband, you should be making sure you take out enough time to rest in order to have the energy to dedicate time for sexual intimacy. Your husband can become resentful of whatever is taking all of your energy when fatigue is the cause of your inability to be intimate with him.

Stress can be a big issue that can dampen your sexual relationship. Worrying, or being preoccupied with things that need to be done can harm your intimate relationship. Try to do things that can help alleviate stress. Believe it or not, sex is actually one of those activities. A well-balanced diet and exercise can be helpful for your mental well-being. In addition, there is communication; and talking about what you're worried about can be helpful. If you communicate with your spouse, he can offer some support that can help alleviate some of the stress.

Other issues can be just problems in other areas of your marriage. Again, communication and resolution of those areas are needed if you want for this area of your marriage to be fulfilling.

Feelings of being unattractive and lack of self-worth can also contribute to dissatisfaction. These are unhealthy feelings, so don't assume that this is just the way things are. Share your feelings with God and with your spouse. Ask the Lord for His guidance. Your husband can only help you if he is aware of your feelings. Share your insecurities with your husband and, if need be, seek the help you need from the Lord, or from your doctor, or a professional counselor.

Spiritual Intimacy

In order for all areas of your marriage to function, including sexual intimacy, you both need to develop a spiritual intimacy as well. Spiritual intimacy is when you and your husband connect together spiritually by seeking God together. If you lack spiritual intimacy, your sexual relationship can also suffer. As a couple you should take time to read the Word together, do devotion together, pray together, and pray for each other, but together. When your husband hears how you pray for him, it can be such an encouragement, and vice-versa.

When you take time to seek the Lord together by doing all these things, you can begin to connect in a powerful way. This is because the Holy Spirit can work with each of you and give each of you compassion and understanding for one another because you are seeking His guidance in your marriage. This spiritual intimacy can help your sexual relationship in a great way.

Through the help of the Holy Spirit you are able to solidify all the other areas of your marriage, making your bond and connection stronger, thereby making your physical intimacy that much stronger as well. Through spiritual intimacy, a tendency to be kinder, more respectful, more forgiving, more patient, more trusting, more tenderhearted, and more communicative will grow stronger.

Make the choice to invite God the Father, God the Son and God the Holy Spirit into every area of your marriage, and not only will your spiritual needs be fulfilled, but your emotional, mental, and physical needs as well.

In Summary

In order for everything to be beautiful on the inside of this project, in order for you to decorate it properly you have to first perform all of the prior steps. Then you must seek God in spiritual intimacy, even more than ever before.

God cares about every area of our lives, including our sexual intimacy with our husband. God wants us to have the best marital relationship we can have and live our marriages in abundance and lacking nothing. We must seek a relationship with Him, do our part in our marital relationship, as well as join together with our husband to place God in the center.

Chapter Five - Discussion Questions

What fears or insecurities you have about yourself, your body, and having sex? What would you like to experience leading up to, and during sexual intimacy?

_____

_____

_____

_____

_____

_____

_____

_____

_____

_____

_____

_____

_____

_____

_____

_____

_____

\Chapter Five – Take Action!

Write a love letter to your husband. Express how much you appreciate his love for you; express what you find most attractive about him; express what his best character and physical features are.

_____

_____

_____

_____

_____

_____

_____

_____

_____

_____

_____

_____

_____

_____

_____

_____

_____

_____

Chapter 6

MAINTENANCE

And this is my prayer: that your love may abound more and more...
Philippians 1:9, NIV

We are finally here! You have reached the final stage of the construction project. However, the final stage can actually be one of the hardest. You have worked hard to get here. You have sought after the Lord, the Architect of this perfect plan, you made sure to lay the strongest foundation possible through communication with the Lord and your spouse. You then moved forward in identifying and learning your role so that you can perform the function that you, and only you were meant to do in this very special project.

The next step you took was not easy, but you did it, you worked together as a team and resolved conflict, and then you were able to have some fun together decorating this beautiful home through some intimate moments with the Lord and each other.

Now it's time for some maintenance. That's right, after you build something you have to maintain it. You want to make sure that what you built is built to last, and the way you do that is by making sure you maintain it. Making sure that you take care of what you put together. It can take lots of hard work, but by making sure you perform some preventative measures, you will not only ensure a life-long strong structure, but you will also make sure that it is here to last throughout generations after you.

When you build a home, you learn to love it more and more each day. But there will be challenges, and you must see through them. Just because you have done everything possible to make sure that everything in your home is perfect, doesn't mean that there won't be times that things go wrong. However, there are ways that you could do some preventative tasks in your home in order to minimize the work.

We have compared marriage relationships throughout this process to a construction project. This was something the Lord laid on my heart, and each step in the construction process is compared to real life marriages. In a real home, you might protect your foundation from damage by installing the correct gutters. You have to service your appliances, service any heating and plumbing systems, and apply fresh paint every now and then, etc.

One way love is demonstrated is through prayer, do you assure your spouse what you prayers are for them?

This is my commandment: Love each other in the same way I have loved you.

John 15:12, NLT

Keeping your Marriage Strong

So it is the same for your marriage. You have to make sure that you are protecting your relationship with God and each other, make sure that you are spending time with each other. Pray together, love each other, and stay committed. You do this through endurance and by being persistent in your intimacy with the Lord and each other. You do this by making sure that you are continuously working together to keep things going strong.

Even after you've worked on improving your marriage, you could still face tough times. You have learned some great ways to strengthen your marriage and to make it better than you could ever imagine. But this doesn't mean that it will be perfect. You still have to work and endure through everything together. Each challenge you face will make you stronger for the next.

Pray continuously for each other, and with each other. You have to be committed to growing spiritually. Even if it is only fifteen minutes a day, you should come together in prayer. You will find that your prayer time together will increase. If you find that you have missed a few days, there is no shame in starting the habit over. Just make sure that you are doing your best to have that moment of prayer.

You must make sacrifices in order to attain a deeper spiritual connection with the Lord. It's only through spiritual growth that

In what ways do you believe that you have grown as a couple?

_____

_____

_____

_____

_____

_____

_____

_____

_____

_____

_____

_____

_____

_____

_____

_____

Dear brothers and sisters, when troubles of any kind come your way, consider it an opportunity for great joy. For you know that when your faith is tested, your endurance has a chance to grow.

James 1:2-3, NLT

you'll be stronger each time you face another challenge. Remember that your marriage is made to reflect Christ and the Church, and you are not to follow the patterns of this world. Instead, know that the Lord who makes everything perfect designed your marriage.

When you are performing maintenance on something, you make sure to perform the required tasks according to the specifications of the instruction manual that came from the manufacturer. Well the Lord is our manufacturer, and His Word is the instruction manual. You need to stay plugged into His manual, and follow His instructions to the letter if you want everything to run smoothly.

Stay plugged into His Word; spend time in devotion with each other. Again, it doesn't have to be for hours. But you should be reading and sharing the Word together. If your spouse is having a difficult time with something, maybe work, with a friend, or anything, it is of great encouragement to give them scripture. I remember that there was a time that I was really going through a rough time, and Luis gave me a scripture that spoke directly to what I was going through. Not only was it helpful, but it brought me more appreciation for my husband because he took the time to look up a scripture that would be of an encouragement to me.

Just as if you would take thoughtful steps to ensure that things don't break down in a home, you should take thoughtful steps so that things don't break down with your spouse and their emotional

How can you sacrifice more time for your spouse?

_____

_____

_____

_____

_____

_____

_____

_____

_____

_____

_____

_____

And so, dear brothers and sisters, I plead with you to give your bodies to God because of all he has done for you. Let them be a living and holy sacrifice—the kind he will find acceptable. This is truly the way to worship him. Don't copy the behavior and customs of this world, but let God transform you into a new person by changing the way you think. Then you will learn to know God's will for you, which is good and pleasing and perfect.

Romans 12:1-2, NLT

being. There are so many challenges that can face each of you individually that can then challenge the unit. Small considerations can make a world of difference.

Built to Last

Another thing is care. When you care for your home, you make sure to make the time to care for it. You have to make time for each other. Life is busy. Most homes have both spouses working in a career. Children can appear and take even more time. Then you have responsibilities with relatives, at church, and with friends. These can monopolize your time.

Life can sometimes get in the way. But, everything that can pull you away from each other will still be waiting even after you have sacrificed some time with each other. Make it a point to spend at least a few hours a week together alone just to relax and have fun. Make an appointment if you have to. It is definitely needed.

When you first got together, you probably tried to spend every waking moment together. It's time to go back to your first love. Remember your first love and take out time for each other. Ensuring that you are taking time to spend with each other cultivating your marriage is important. Second only to spending time with the Lord, this is one of the most important things you can do. Make sure to make plans for date night. Whether it is a night

Determine how you can make more time for God's Word.

_____

_____

_____

_____

_____

_____

_____

_____

_____

_____

_____

_____

_____

_____

_____

_____

Your word is a lamp to guide my feet and a light for my path.
Psalms 119:105, NLT

out on the town, or a quiet time alone at home, you need to take the time to be together. Take the time to talk, to laugh, and to share. This will strengthen your marriage.

Luis and I are not quite there yet, but soon we will be empty nesters. You may be going through this time right now. This time of your life is different, but I know that it can also be great. With children gone, so many thoughts and feelings can get in the way. Your children monopolized your time for so many years, that now you have to try to have other things to continue to connect you. This is where your intimate relationship and strong communication can help.

When it's just the two of you, whether it's new, or it has always been that way, you continually have to take time to cultivate your marriage. You want what you have built together to last a lifetime. The best way to do this is time. Whether you are newly married, or whether you have been married for years, time together will only build your marriage stronger. When moments get rough, the time you have spent together will help the rough times. When you are older, the amount of time you invested in your marriage is what is going to help you get through anything and keep your bond unbreakable.

I know that this can be difficult, and sometimes a challenge, but it is necessary. Many things can get in the way. Finances are one thing that can be a challenge, but there are free and other cost-efficient ways to spend time together. The important thing is that you both understand your finances, and plan with your budget in mind. However, I do suggest that every now and then you treat yourself in doing something you both really want and make the sacrifice to invest money into that time. It's an investment that you won't regret.

Another thing concerning time, is time itself. Just because the years have set in and you are comfortable with each other doesn't mean that you can't try to be spontaneous every once in awhile. In a home, sometimes you do a makeover, and make changes to keep the home looking fresh and beautiful. Well, it's the same for your marriage. A fresh coat of paint, new curtains, and other touches make your home look great. Even if it's the same color of paint, your home can look brand new. Well, for your marriage it's the same.

Husbands, do something surprising for your wife. Just like the same paint, even if it's something that you've done for her when you were first together, you can make her happy. Wives, surprises are not only for husbands to do, you can certainly do something spontaneous for your husband. Small considerations go a long way. There is no shame in taking on the role of romancing your husband.

Try something new. New hobbies, and adventures can be helpful to build new memories. Sometimes holding on to the ways things used to be can be damaging. Don't get me wrong, it is great to remember the old times, and to re-live memories, but making new memories is even better. We all need times of fun and laughter. Times to try things that will spark up new interests. Building and rebuilding repeatedly can be great.

Another helpful thing is to show interest in what your spouse has interest in. Luis loves sports. So, I often watch sports with him. This shows him that I care about what interests him. Luis does the same. He takes time to do things with me that I love. If your husband likes fishing, go fishing with him. If your wife likes romantic movies, watch them with her. I know some of these things may seem simple, but it is the simple things, that we can take for granted and pay no mind to its importance.

If one of you are the social bug and likes to entertain and invite friends over, then the other should be willing to have these times in support of the other. If it makes them happy, then go ahead and let them entertain. But, this also works in reverse. If one of you is not that social, then try to limit how often you entertain and have others over. Give and take. Don't confuse this with 50/50. This is actually 100/100.

You are both sacrificing fully in and every way possible for the interests of the other. Eventually this becomes continuous and should one day not be such a sacrifice. It would be nice for the time to come that you both enjoy the mere fact that you are making one another happy and content with the things that you do together.

I recall that when Luis and I were first married, he would stay in another room when I had people over. This would bother me so much. I felt that it was rude, and felt that it made people feel as though as they were not welcomed. I loved entertaining. I never fought with him about it.

When his family was over, I was tempted to do the same thing and kind of give him a taste of his own medicine, but I never did that. Instead, I acted with his family and friends the way I would have loved him to act when I had people over. I did communicate how I felt about it with him, and at first, he didn't do much to change. But as time passed, he started to do a bit more and more to be present when I had family or friends over.

As time passed, and as his relationship grew with the Lord, his love for people also began to grow. What's amazing is that today we are both the same in that respect. He also loves to entertain, and is often very considerate about the details of how we entertain. He wants to make people feel comfortable and at home. If he knows something about our guests, he makes sure to supply what they like for them when they are over, such as a favorite dessert, or a favorite game.

Luis did a total 180-degree turn. He is completely different. This is mainly because his relationship with the Lord helped his love for people grow, but also because he took the time to try to make me happy in this area. This is a great example of sacrificing something that eventually became a joy and not such a sacrifice as well. Time and sacrifice will help your marriage last a lifetime.

Built to Last for your Children

You want your marriage to not only last throughout your lifetime, but also to be a testament to what God can do for generations to come. One way this happens is through your children, and through others. To be the prime example for your children, you can demonstrate a healthy, strong, God-filled, and God-inspired individual life and marriage.

Men, as the head of the household, you want to make sure that your children are staying grounded in the Word, and that they are learning to be fighters for their marriage. That they are learning to follow God's plan and design. You want your boys to follow your example to be a God-fearing husband and father. You want your grandchildren in the care of the best. Your sons should learn from you how to love God, how to lead their home, how to honor, trust, love and care for their wife, and how to love and care for their children. They should learn from you how to pray and keep their family united. But, best of all, how to keep their family in the Lord. So, when the time comes for your sons to begin a marital relationship, you know that you have armed them with the best lessons and tools to have a great marriage.

You are the first example for your sons. However, you are also the best example for your daughters as well. You will be showing your daughters what they should look for in a husband by the way

In what ways can you sacrifice for the joy of your spouse?

...But as for me and my family, we will serve the Lord.
Joshua 24:15, NLT

you treat your wife. You are your daughters' first example of what a husband should do for her, the way a husband should act with her, and the way a husband should love her.

You want your daughters to be treated in the best way, so therefore you are to set that example by treating your wife the way you would want your daughters to be treated. Your daughters will know to look for a husband who will love her sacrificially, and who will trust, honor and respect her. There is a saying that daughters will marry men like their fathers. Dad, you set the standard. How high would you set it when it concerns the future of your daughters?

Women, as the important helper, you too want to make sure that your children stay grounded in the Word. You want to nurture them, also show them to fight for their marriages. You are the first example to your daughters, and will show them what it is to be a Godly wife and mother.

Your daughters will learn from you how to establish and build their own homes through seeking wisdom from the Lord. Your daughters will learn about being grounded in the Word, and knowing their value in their relationships. They will know all that they need to know about strengthening their marriage through what you show them. They will learn how to teach and nurture their children as well.

You are also the first examples to your sons. You will show your sons what type of wife they should marry. You will show

What kind of example do you want to be? In what ways can you influence others?

...indeed, I have a beautiful inheritance.

Psalms 16:6, ESV

them how they should expect to be loved, honored and respected by their future wives. You are the first example of what type of wife they want to look for.

I am sure that you want your sons to be treated in the best way, so you set that example by treating your husband the way you would want your sons to be treated. Your sons will know to look for a wife who will love them sacrificially, and who will trust, honor and respect them. There is also a saying that sons will marry women like their mothers. Mom, you set the standard. How high would you set it when it concerns the future of your sons?

When you apply the Word of God in your marriage and do your best to live by it, you are not only saving your marriage, you are helping to establish a good foundation for the marriages of your children. You are placing in them the ability to distinguish between what the world has to say about marriage and what God says about marriage. You are allowing them to see that God's way is the best way, when you choose to make God's way the only way for your marriage. You are leaving them an inheritance that will be beautiful for you.

When your children go through challenges in their marriage, they will think about how you handled some of the same tough situations. You're ensuring that they will look for healthy relationships, and that they will seek good counsel, including yours. Who better to advise your own children other than yourself? No other person cares for them, or wants better for them, than you.

Do you have healthy relationships with other couples? Name some that you may be interested in building a friendship, and then make a point to do it.

Remember the days of long ago; think about the generations past. Ask your father, and he will inform you. Inquire of your elders, and they will tell you.

Deuteronomy 32:7, NLT

It will bless you to know that not only did you do your best in your marriage and as parents, but that your best was acknowledged and was a good example for your children. Your children will know to seek your advice because of the example that you have given them. Then your children will influence their children and so forth. The life you lead in God now, will affect the generations to come. Raising children in a healthy environment will give them the best fighting chance at having future healthy families as well.

Built to Last as a Testament for Others

Another way that you will ensure that your testament will last past generations is your ability to affect other marriages as well. Through God, you can inspire your friends and their marriages. I have learned about breakups and divorces that have happened to good friends and it hurts when it happens.

But I have also seen Luis and I influence the marriages of other friends, and when we do, it is such a blessing to us that we were able to help. For us, this is a passion, and we want to see marriages changed near and far. It doesn't necessarily have to be a passion for you, but I am sure that you would love to positively affect the lives of those you care about and are close to you.

When you love Jesus and allow Him to reflect Himself in your marriage, you can affect others. You can testify to how Jesus has helped your marriage stay strong through the years by keeping Him in the center. Throughout the years, Luis and I have always reached out to other couples. We try to spark a friendship and fellowship with them for a number of reasons. For one, we love people! We want to build relationships with people. It is so great to get to know other couples and hear their point of view and their stories.

It is good to find other Godly couples that you can bond with. It can be a great encouragement for your marriage. Good friendships help with stress, and help you grow your perspective with each other. When you are able to identify yourselves with other couples and see that you are normal with your issues, they become a little bit easier to face. You understand that you are not alone, that you are not the only couple that faces the types of challenges you face. This is important because a lie that the enemy often likes to use is that your relationship is in the worst shape, or that your relationship is abnormal, when in fact it's not.

Just like young children or teenagers, we also need to hang out with others. We laugh together and we learn from them just as much as they learn from us. This helps us in our marriage and it helps them. It is so great to bond with others that have the same faith, and are fighting the same battles. Don't be mistaken, most marriages face the same type of issues daily, and with good friendships you may not only help others, but you'll learn as well.

Conclusion

This has been quite a building project, and living out the information that you may have learned can help you tremendously. Keeping Christ in the center of your life, your marriage, and your family is the best action you can take. No one else can do for you as God does. But through that close relationship, change has to take hold of your life and you have to ensure that you are living an obedient life in the Lord. Obedience to His Word will lead you into the right path, and into the best life that you can possibly have.

Luis and I have tried our best to share with you all the concepts that we have learned through years of experience and straight from God's Word. This is because it is only through God's Word that you will live out the life and marriage that God intended for you. We challenge you today to put into practice the things we have shared with you in your marriage. We believe that when you do, you will not be disappointed.

Your marriage will be a marriage that was built to last!

Chapter Six - Discussion Questions

What are some things you could do for your husband, and places that you could go together, that he would enjoy?

_____

_____

_____

_____

_____

_____

_____

_____

_____

_____

_____

_____

_____

_____

_____

Chapter Six – Take Action!

Take some time to pray aloud together, expressing gratitude for specific things about each other that you're thankful for. Ask God to give you strength and wisdom to work on yourselves, both individually and as a couple. And Thank Him for the blessings in your marriage, both current, and those yet to come.

Final Assignment

Together with your husband, pick something to do, or a place to go from your list on page 197. Then make it happen!

_____

_____

_____

_____

_____

_____

_____

_____

_____

_____

Find additional resources at **http://www.remodelministries.org**

Luis & Angela Hernandez, Remodel Ministries

As the leaders of this ministry Luis and Angela have a passion for carefully unpacking the truths of Scripture. They understand the power to change lives that emanates from the Scriptures. They have served in several ministries and capacities for over ten years, including recently leading a local marriage ministry. They have been married for over twenty years and have three children.

You can contact them at angela@remodelministries.org, or luis@remodelministries.org.

Made in the USA
Columbia, SC
10 December 2018